THE
TOFU
COOKBOOK

HEATHER THOMAS

THE
TOFU
COOKBOOK

HEATHER THOMAS

EBURY
PRESS

CONTENTS

MAIN MEALS

BAKING & DESSERTS

INTRODUCTION

Tofu has become one of the highest trending go-to foods in recent years as more of us are embracing a healthier, meat-free way of eating. It is made by pressing the curds of fermented fresh soya milk (derived from soya beans) into soft, white solid blocks. It's a staple ingredient in Japanese, Thai and Chinese cookery and, depending on how it is cooked, it can be crisp and crunchy or soft and creamy. Its subtle, neutral flavour lends itself to both sweet and savoury dishes, making it a very versatile food.

Tofu was first made in China about 2,000 years ago and was introduced into Japan in the eighth century. However, it did not arrive in the West until the 1960s when people became more interested in vegetarian food, healthy eating and experimenting with exotic and unfamiliar cuisines. Now more people than ever are eating vegetarian and/or vegan options several times a week, as plant-based eating is taking the health world by storm and there's a fundamental shift in our eating habits. The appeal of tofu has extended far beyond vegans, to encompass everyone who is interested in eating a healthier and more sustainable diet with benefits linked to animal ethics and the environment.

NUTRITION & HEALTH

Tofu is a good source of protein and contains all eight essential amino acids (making it especially valuable for vegetarians) as well as the essential minerals iron, calcium, manganese, selenium, phosphorus, magnesium, copper, zinc and vitamin B1. In addition, it's gluten-free, cholesterol-free and low-calorie.

Soya protein is believed to help lower the bad cholesterol LDL (low-density lipoprotein) in the body. It contains phytoestrogens, which are compounds that occur naturally in plants and are similar to the female hormone oestrogen. This makes tofu a popular food for many menopausal and older women whose bodies have stopped producing oestrogen.

TYPES OF TOFU

Tofu is available in several different forms – each having its own distinctive texture and consistency, depending on the water content. The more water it contains, the silkier and softer the tofu; the less water, the firmer it is.

SILKEN TOFU is unpressed and has a high water content and a very fine, soft and creamy texture – similar to burrata cheese. You can use it as a thick cream when making desserts, cakes and soup. It can also be blended into sauces, dressings and smoothies. It does not usually need refrigeration. Just drain it before using.

SOFT TOFU absorbs the flavours of sauces and broths and is used in stews, desserts, shakes, spreads, sauces, salad dressings and 'scrambles'. Soft tofu must be kept in the fridge.

FIRM TOFU is very versatile and often packaged soaked in liquid. It has the consistency of feta cheese and is usually pressed (see page 10) to extract the moisture before baking, frying or using as a filling. Store firm tofu in the fridge.

EXTRA-FIRM TOFU does not absorb marinades as well as firm tofu but it is easier to pan-fry, deep-fry and stir-fry and to achieve a crisp golden crust. Use it for griddling, grilling (broiling) and baking. Extra-firm tofu should be stored in the fridge and it usually needs pressing before using (see page 10).

FLAVOURED TOFU

In addition to plain tofu there's an increasing variety of ready-flavoured tofus available to buy from health stores and supermarkets.

SMOKED TOFU has a distinctive savoury flavour – it's usually smoked over beech wood. It is extra-firm and is often used pan-fried or eaten raw in salads, sliced in sandwiches or for topping veggie burgers.

MARINATED TOFU is usually spiced, ready to cook and requires no preparation. Marinated tofu can be firm or extra-firm.

CHOOSING & STORING TOFU

Tofu is now widely available in most large supermarkets as well as specialist health food stores and from online retailers. If possible, always choose GM-free tofu made from 100 per cent organic soya beans with no additives.

When opened, firm and extra-firm tofu needs to be rinsed, covered with water and kept in a sealed container in the fridge. It will stay fresh for up to one week if the water is changed frequently. If kept in the original package it will freeze for up to six months.

COOKING WITH TOFU

Because tofu is a blank canvas with a rather bland and subtle flavour, seasoning, marinating and/or coating it with seeds, herbs, spices, fruit juice, aromatics, vinegar, oil and hot sauces will enhance its taste and transform it into a delicious snack or meal. Texture matters, too, especially when it is seared, griddled or fried. A really crispy golden crust complemented by a creamy interior makes all the difference.

This book will show you not only how to prepare tofu but also how to season, marinate and flavour it to get the best results. It is amazingly versatile and as well as the traditional Chinese, Japanese and Thai dishes where it's the dominant ingredient, we feature tofu recipes from around the world. We feature a selection of delicious snacks, dips, dressings, homemade mayo, smoothies and sauces, plus breakfast and brunch dishes, salads, sandwiches, lunches, main meals and even a chapter devoted to desserts and baking with tofu.

NOTE FOR VEGETARIANS & VEGANS

All the recipes in this book are suitable for vegetarians and many are vegan-friendly, too. Vegans can easily adapt most of the dishes that feature dairy products by substituting dairy-free products, such as nut or soya milk alternatives, dairy-free yoghurt alternatives and vegan cheese-style blocks. Where honey is specified, use agave or maple syrup instead.

BASIC TOFU RECIPES

We know that tofu is very nutritious and good for us but how do we make it taste really good? It has such a subtle, if not bland, flavour that how it's cooked makes all the difference. If you've never prepared or cooked tofu before, don't worry – it's very quick and easy. Just follow the basic instructions here.

PRESSING FIRM OR EXTRA-FIRM TOFU

Most of the recipes in this book using firm or extra-firm tofu specify pressed tofu. Because it contains water and is packed in water, it soaks some of it up like a sponge and needs pressing to extract it. This is the key to achieving a really crisp, golden brown exterior and a tender, moist interior when stir-frying or pan-frying tofu, so it's very important that you know how to press it. Just follow the simple instructions below:

1 Remove the block of tofu from the packing water/liquid and drain it.

2 Cut the block into 2.5cm/1in slices and place them in a single layer between 2 sheets of kitchen paper (paper towel) on a plate. Cover with a clean cloth and put some heavy cans or books on top.

3 Leave for at least 30 minutes and then drain the water. You can leave it for 1–2 hours if wished, draining off the water several times.

4 Use the sliced tofu or cut into cubes or dice and proceed with the recipe.

NOTE: You can press the whole block of tofu in the same way but it will take longer to extract the water.

FLAVOURING TOFU

Tofu has a very mild and indistinct flavour, especially after pressing, so many recipes call for marinating or seasoning before you cook it.

MARINATING TOFU

Avoid using oil, which can prevent the flavourings penetrating the tofu. Choose from strong-tasting and piquant flavourings such as vinegar, citrus juice (lemon, lime or orange), soy sauce, tamari, barbecue sauce and vegetable stock (broth). You can also add herbs, crushed garlic, diced chilli and ground spices to the marinade.

SEASONING TOFU

Simply sprinkle over freshly ground black pepper and salt or dried or finely chopped fresh herbs and ground spices. Rub the seasoning into the tofu for the best flavour.

COATING TOFU

Plain, seasoned or marinated firm and extra-firm tofu can be coated before stir-frying or pan-frying. This will not only make it crispy but will also help prevent it sticking to the pan. You can use plain (all-purpose) flour or cornflour (cornstarch) but go easy on it and shake off any excess – you only need a light coating. Alternatively, for additional texture and flavour, use white or black sesame seeds or five-spice powder.

1 Sprinkle the flour in a thin layer in a shallow dish or baking tray.

2 Place the tofu on top and gently turn it in the flour until it is coated all over.

NOTE: You can also coat the tofu in batter (see the recipe on page 79).

COOKING TOFU

There are many ways of cooking firm and extra-firm tofu, including stir-frying, pan-frying, deep-frying, baking, griddling, grilling (broiling) and cooking over hot coals on a barbecue.

PAN-FRYING AND STIR-FRYING
You don't need a lot of vegetable oil, so just spray the pan lightly and when it's really hot, add the tofu and cook until golden brown on both sides. Drain the fried tofu on kitchen paper (paper towels) before serving.

DEEP-FRYING
Cubed tofu can be coated with flour or cornflour (cornstarch) and deep-fried until golden brown all over and crisp on the outside but soft on the inside. Always drain the deep-fried tofu on kitchen paper (paper towels) before serving.

GRIDDLING, GRILLING (BROILING) AND BARBECUING
Lightly spray a hot griddle, grill (broiler) tray or barbecue rack with oil. Add the tofu and cook until golden brown or attractively striped.

BAKING
Tofu, sliced or cubed, is best baked at 200°C, 400°F, gas mark 6. You can marinate or coat it before placing it in a single layer on a baking tray (cookie sheet) lined with baking parchment. Bake, turning halfway through, until golden brown.

NOTE: Cubes of tofu are approximately 2–2.5cm/1in, unless otherwise stated.

SUPER-CRISP FRIED TOFU

SERVES: 4 AS A LIGHT MEAL OR STARTER | **PREP:** 10 MINUTES | **STAND:** 30-35 MINUTES
COOK: 4-6 MINUTES

~~~~~~~~~~~~~~~~~~~~~~~~~~~~

450g/1lb firm or extra-firm tofu, cut into cubes
1 tbsp vegetable oil, plus extra for deep-frying
2 garlic cloves, thinly sliced
1 red bird's eye chilli, deseeded and diced
4 spring onions (scallions), thinly sliced
salt and freshly ground black pepper

OR YOU CAN TRY THIS...

– Lightly coat the tofu cubes with cornflour (cornstarch) or flour before frying.
– Add some finely sliced fresh root ginger or lemongrass to the fried garlic and chilli mixture.
– Serve with a soy dipping sauce or drizzle with sweet chilli sauce.

You can use any lightly flavoured vegetable oil, such as sunflower or very light olive oil, for frying the tofu. Don't omit the boiling step. It may sound bizarre but it will make the finished dish crispier.

1 Bring some salted water to the boil in a saucepan. Add the tofu and remove from the heat immediately. Set aside for 15 minutes, then drain well.

2 Place the tofu in a single layer on a baking tray (cookie sheet) lined with kitchen paper (paper towels). Cover with more kitchen paper and a tea towel and weight with heavy cans or books. Press for 15–20 minutes, then drain on kitchen paper.

3 Heat 1 tablespoon vegetable oil in a small non-stick frying pan (skillet) over a medium to high heat and stir-fry the garlic, chilli and spring onions for 1–2 minutes without browning. Remove immediately with a slotted spoon and drain on kitchen paper.

4 Meanwhile, heat the oil for deep-frying in a large heavy-based saucepan (it should be at least 5cm/2in deep) or deep fat fryer until it reaches 180°C/350°F. Either use a sugar thermometer to check the temperature or add a cube of bread – the oil is ready when the bread cube sizzles and turns brown in 25 seconds.

5 Add the drained tofu cubes to the hot oil and cook for about 3–4 minutes, or until crisp and golden all over (you may have to do this in batches, depending on the size of the pan). Remove with a slotted spoon and drain on kitchen paper.

6 Season with salt and pepper and serve sprinkled with the fried garlic, chilli and spring onions.

~~~~~~~~~~~~~~~~~~~~~~~~~~~~

SNACKS & DRINKS

SILKEN TOFU HUMMUS

SERVES: 4 | **PREP:** 10 MINUTES

115g/4oz silken tofu
50g/2oz (½ cup) canned
    chickpeas, rinsed and
    drained, plus extra
    to garnish
4 tbsp tahini
2 garlic cloves, crushed
4 tbsp extra virgin olive oil,
    plus extra for drizzling
juice of 1 lemon
salt and freshly ground
    black pepper
paprika or cayenne pepper,
    for sprinkling
warm pitta bread fingers,
    to serve

If you've never considered adding tofu to hummus, think again. Not only does it make it more nutritious by boosting the protein content but it's also delicious and more creamy than regular hummus.

1 Put the tofu, chickpeas, tahini, garlic, olive oil and lemon juice in a blender. Blitz until you have a thick and creamy mixture. If it's too thick, thin it with a little water or more olive oil. Season to taste with salt and pepper.

2 Transfer the hummus to a serving bowl, top with some whole chickpeas and drizzle with olive oil. Sprinkle lightly with paprika or cayenne pepper and serve with warm pitta bread fingers.

OR YOU CAN TRY THIS...
– Add some ground cumin or coriander and some dried or chopped fresh herbs, such as marjoram, oregano, basil or coriander (cilantro).
– Roast the garlic cloves before blitzing.
– Add a diced hot chilli.
– Serve with raw vegetable sticks, tortilla chips or savoury crackers.

SMOKED TOFU SATAY

SERVES: 4 | **PREP:** 15 MINUTES | **COOK:** 4-5 MINUTES

For the peanut butter dip:
150g/5oz (generous ½ cup)
    crunchy peanut butter
60g/2oz creamed coconut,
    grated
1 garlic clove, crushed
juice of 1 lime
2 tbsp soy sauce
2 tbsp sweet chilli sauce

For the satay:
250g/9oz firm smoked tofu,
    pressed (see page 10)
2 tbsp cornflour (cornstarch)
¼ tsp smoked paprika
vegetable oil for deep-frying
coarse sea salt and freshly
    ground black pepper

You can make the peanut butter dip in advance but the deep-fried tofu should be eaten really hot to enjoy it at its crispy best. If you don't have any peanut butter, just serve the skewers with some bottled sweet chilli sauce.

1 For the dip, stir together the peanut butter, coconut, garlic, lime juice, soy sauce and sweet chilli sauce. Thin to the desired dipping consistency with 1–2 tablespoons cold water and set aside.

2 Cut the drained, pressed tofu into 8 cubes and toss gently in the cornflour and paprika, until lightly coated all over.

3 Heat the oil in a non-stick wok or wide heavy-based pan set over a high heat. When it's really hot, add the tofu, using some tongs or a slotted spoon. Fry for 4–5 minutes until crisp and golden. Remove carefully and drain on kitchen paper (paper towels).

4 While the tofu is still very hot, sprinkle with salt and pepper and thread onto 4 small wooden or bamboo skewers. Serve immediately with the peanut butter dip.

OR YOU CAN TRY THIS...

– Serve with griddled whole spring onions (scallions) and some boiled rice.
– Sprinkle the hot fried tofu with diced red chilli or some crushed chilli flakes.

TOFU SUMMER ROLLS

MAKES: 8 ROLLS | **PREP:** 20 MINUTES | **COOK:** 20 MINUTES

200g/7oz firm tofu, pressed
  (see page 10)
2 tbsp hoisin sauce
juice of ½ lime
1 garlic clove, crushed
1 tbsp sunflower oil
1 red (bell) pepper,
  deseeded and cut into
  thin matchsticks
1 large carrot, cut into thin
  matchsticks
2.5cm/1in piece fresh root
  ginger, peeled and diced
85g/3oz spring greens,
  shredded
85g/3oz (¾ cup)
  beansprouts
2 tbsp light soy sauce
a handful of coriander
  (cilantro), chopped
8 round rice paper wrappers
hoisin sauce or sweet chilli
  sauce, to serve

These Vietnamese-style summer rolls look really impressive but they are very easy to make. Enjoy them as a healthy snack or as an appetiser. You can buy rice paper wrappings in Asian stores, delis and many supermarkets.

1 Preheat the oven to 180°C, 350°F, gas mark 4. Line a baking tray (cookie sheet) with baking parchment.

2 Cut the block of tofu lengthways into 16 long thin strips. Mix together the hoisin sauce, lime juice and garlic and brush over the tofu strips. Arrange them on the lined baking tray.

3 Bake the tofu for about 20 minutes, turning halfway through, until crisp and browned all over on the outside.

4 Meanwhile, heat the oil in a non-stick wok or frying pan (skillet) and stir fry the red pepper, carrot and ginger for 2 minutes. Add the spring greens and beansprouts and cook for 2 minutes. Stir in the soy sauce and coriander.

5 Dip a rice paper wrapper into a bowl of cold water until it's pliable. Lay it out flat on a clean work surface and top with one-eighth of the stir fried vegetables, leaving a wide border around the edge. Place 2 tofu strips on top. Fold the sides of the wrapper over the filling to enclose it and then roll up tightly like a parcel. Repeat with the rest of the wrappers, vegetables and tofu.

6 Serve the rolls, drizzled with hoisin sauce or sweet chilli sauce.

OR YOU CAN TRY THIS...
– Add some vermicelli rice noodles or cellophane noodles to the filling.
– Vary the vegetables, using cucumber strips and spring onions (scallions).
– Add some chopped roasted peanuts or cashews.
– Serve with peanut butter dip (see page 19).

CRISPY BAKED TOFU BITES

SERVES: 4 | **PREP:** 10 MINUTES | **COOK:** 25-30 MINUTES

For the tofu bites:
350g/12oz extra-firm
    or firm tofu, pressed
    (see page 10)
1 tbsp soy sauce
2 tbsp cornflour (cornstarch)
freshly ground black pepper
sesame seeds, for sprinkling

For the honey soy sauce:
2 tbsp clear honey
1 tbsp soy sauce
juice of ½ lime
2 garlic cloves, crushed

You can serve these delicious and versatile bites as a snack or appetiser or even as a light meal with stir-fried greens or Tenderstem® broccoli and some boiled rice or quinoa.

1 Preheat the oven to 200°C, 400°F, gas mark 6. Line a baking tray (cookie sheet) with baking parchment.

2 Cut the pressed tofu into cubes and toss in the soy sauce in a bowl. Transfer to another bowl and toss in the cornflour until lightly coated. Place the tofu on the lined baking tray.

3 Bake the tofu for 25–30 minutes, turning halfway through, until crisp and golden brown all over.

4 Meanwhile, put all the ingredients for the honey soy sauce in a small saucepan and set over a medium heat. Heat gently, stirring occasionally, until hot and slightly thickened. Remove from the heat.

5 Serve the tofu, sprinkled with black pepper and sesame seeds, with the hot honey soy sauce.

OR YOU CAN TRY THIS...
– Pan-fry or deep-fry the tofu cubes instead of baking.
– Use agave syrup instead of honey in the sauce.
– Substitute lemon juice for lime juice.
– Add some diced fresh chilli or crushed dried chilli flakes.

TLT SANDWICH

SERVES: 4 | **PREP:** 15 MINUTES | **COOK:** 4-8 MINUTES

400g/14oz extra-firm tofu, pressed (see page 10)

2 tbsp cornflour (cornstarch)

2 tbsp sunflower oil

8 slices wholegrain or multi-seed bread

1 ripe avocado, peeled, stoned (pitted) and mashed

4 tbsp vegan mayo

2 ripe tomatoes, sliced

Sriracha sauce, for drizzling (optional)

a few crisp cos (romaine) or iceberg lettuce leaves

salt and freshly ground black pepper

We've all heard of the BLT sandwich but here's a delicious vegan version – the TLT, made with tofu, lettuce and tomato.

1 Cut the tofu into 8–12 slices and dust them with cornflour. Season lightly with salt and pepper.

2 Heat the oil in a large non-stick frying pan (skillet) set over a medium heat and cook the tofu, in batches (do not overcrowd the pan), for 1–2 minutes each side until crisp and golden. Remove with a slotted spoon and drain on kitchen paper (paper towels).

3 Lightly toast the bread and spread 4 slices with the mashed avocado and the remaining slices with the vegan mayo.

4 Arrange the sliced tomatoes over the avocado and top with the hot fried tofu. Drizzle with Sriracha sauce, if using, and cover with the lettuce. Top with the remaining toasted bread and cut the sandwiches in half or into quarters. Serve immediately.

OR YOU CAN TRY THIS...

– Marinate the tofu before frying for additional flavour.

– Add some roasted vegetables.

TOFU PROTEIN SMOOTHIE

SERVES: 1 | **PREP:** 5 MINUTES

175g/6oz silken tofu
1 small banana
85g/3oz (¾ cup) blueberries
3 tbsp soy protein powder
a few drops of vanilla
   extract
240ml/8fl oz (1 cup)
   cold unsweetened soya
   milk alternative
ice (optional)

Get your day off to a good start with this delicious tofu and blueberry smoothie. It's packed with protein and so quick and easy to make.

1 Put all the ingredients, except the ice, in a blender and blitz until smooth.

2 Pour into a tall glass and drink immediately, adding ice if wished.

OR YOU CAN TRY THIS...

– If you have a sweet tooth, add honey or maple syrup, to taste.
– Use almond milk alternative and almond extract instead of soya milk alternative and vanilla extract.
– Add some chia seeds or stoned (pitted) dates.
– Vary the berries according to what's in season.

TOFU, NUT BUTTER & HONEY SMOOTHIE

SERVES: 1 | **PREP:** 5 MINUTES

1 frozen banana
115g/4oz soft or silken tofu
2 tbsp almond butter
120ml/4fl oz (½ cup)
    almond milk alternative
2 tsp clear honey
a few drops of almond
    extract (optional)

You can make this shake as thick or as runny as you like by varying the amount of milk alternative. Don't worry if you don't have a frozen banana – just use a ripe one at room temperature and add some crushed ice.

1 Put all the ingredients in a blender and blitz until smooth. If the milkshake is too thick for your liking, just add some more milk and blitz again.

2 Pour into a tall glass and serve immediately.

OR YOU CAN TRY THIS...
– Use maple syrup instead of honey
– Add a pinch of ground cinnamon.
– Add 1 tablespoon cocoa powder for a chocolate flavour.
– Use soya or rice milk alternatives instead of almond milk alternative.
– Substitute peanut butter for almond butter.

STRAWBERRY TOFU SHAKE

SERVES: 1 | **PREP:** 5 MINUTES

115g/4oz soft or silken tofu
200g/7oz fresh strawberries,
   hulled (stems removed)
120ml/4fl oz (½ cup) soya
   milk alternative
2 tsp clear honey or agave
   syrup

This breakfast drink has the consistency of a shake rather than a classic fruit smoothie. If it's too thick for you, add some more soya milk alternative. It stores well in the fridge, so you could double the quantity and save half for tomorrow.

1 Put all the ingredients in a blender and blitz until smooth.

2 Pour into a tall glass and serve immediately, or cover and chill in the fridge for up to 2 days.

OR YOU CAN TRY THIS...

– Use raspberries or blueberries instead of strawberries.
– If you don't have a sweet tooth, omit the honey or agave syrup and add a dash of lemon juice.
– Use maple syrup instead of honey or agave syrup.

LIGHT MEALS & SALADS

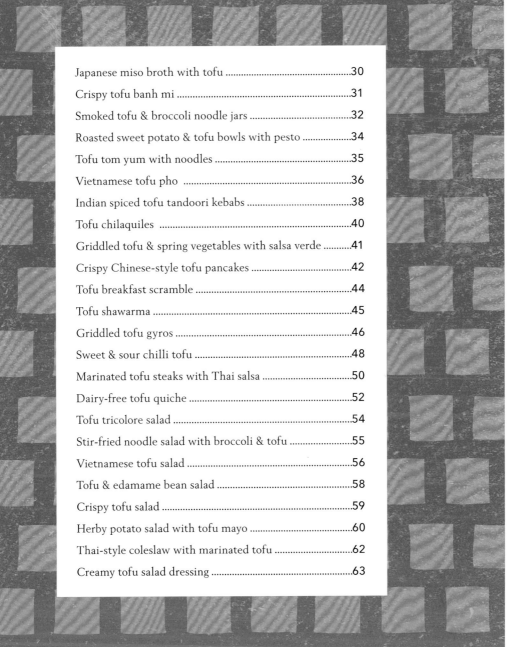

JAPANESE MISO BROTH WITH TOFU

SERVES: 4-6 | **PREP:** 5 MINUTES | **STAND:** 10-15 MINUTES | **COOK:** 15 MINUTES

1 tbsp dried wakame
  seaweed flakes
1.2 litres/2 pints (5 cups)
  vegetable stock (broth)
4 tbsp white miso paste
2 garlic cloves, thinly sliced
1 tsp grated fresh root
  ginger
1 bunch of spring onions
  (scallions), thinly sliced
1 large carrot, cut into thin
  matchsticks
200g/7oz thin asparagus,
  trimmed and sliced
1 pak choi (bok choy),
  trimmed and leaves
  separated
225g/8oz silken tofu,
  cut into cubes
soy sauce (optional)

This delicious cleansing broth is so quick and easy to make and will warm you up on a cold winter's day. Use homemade stock, if possible, for the best flavour, but good-quality organic bouillon cubes or powder work well, too.

1 Put the wakame flakes in a bowl and cover with plenty of cold water. Leave for 10–15 minutes until soft and rehydrated. Drain well.

2 Pour the stock into a large saucepan and bring to the boil. Reduce the heat to a simmer and add the miso paste. Stir with a wooden spoon until it dissolves.

3 Add the garlic, ginger, spring onions, carrot and asparagus and simmer gently for 4–5 minutes. Stir in the pak choi and cook for 2–3 minutes. Add the drained wakame and tofu and heat through gently for 1 minute. Check the seasoning, adding some soy sauce to taste, if wished.

4 Ladle the soup into serving bowls and serve immediately.

OR YOU CAN TRY THIS...

– Add some shredded greens or sliced shiitake or enoki mushrooms.
– Stir in some chopped herbs, e.g. coriander (cilantro), mint or basil.
– Add a shredded red bird's eye chilli.
– Drizzle in a beaten egg at the end (just before serving) and stir with a fork for about 2 minutes until it forms long strands.
– Add some thin noodles.

CRISPY TOFU BANH MI

SERVES: 4 | **PREP:** 20 MINUTES | **STAND:** AT LEAST 1 HOUR | **COOK:** 10 MINUTES

For the spicy mayo:
120g/4oz (½ cup) vegan
    mayonnaise
2 spring onions (scallions),
    diced
2 tbsp hot sauce, e.g. Sriracha
    or sweet chilli sauce

For the baguettes:
2 carrots, cut into thin
    matchsticks
4 radishes, thinly sliced
1 red (bell) pepper,
    deseeded and thinly
    sliced
1 small ridged cucumber,
    thinly sliced
4 tbsp rice vinegar
4 tbsp caster (superfine)
    sugar
1 tbsp soy sauce or nam pla
    (Thai fish sauce)
1–2 tbsp vegetable oil
400g/14oz firm or extra-
    firm tofu, pressed
    (see page 10) and cut
    into cubes
4 small baguettes
    (French sticks)
1 red onion, thinly sliced
a handful of coriander
    (cilantro), chopped

This delicious 'sandwich' takes longer to make than most but it's worth it. If you can't get small baguettes, just buy a really long one and cut it into sections.

1 Make the spicy mayo: mix all the ingredients together in a bowl. Cover and leave in the fridge until you're ready to assemble the baguettes.

2 Mix together the carrots, radishes, red pepper and cucumber in a glass bowl. Heat the vinegar and sugar in a small saucepan, stirring until the sugar dissolves, then bring to the boil and remove from the heat. Stir in the soy sauce and pour over the vegetables. Leave to marinate for at least 1 hour.

3 Just before you're ready to eat, heat the oil in a large non-stick frying pan (skillet) set over a medium to high heat. Add the tofu and cook, turning occasionally, for 4–5 minutes until golden and crisp all over. Remove and drain on kitchen paper (paper towels).

4 Split the baguettes in half lengthways and scoop out some of the soft bread in the centre to leave a crusty shell. Spread the spicy mayo over the bases and then add the tofu. Top with the carrot and radish mixture and the sliced red onion and coriander. Cover with the baguette tops, pressing down firmly. Eat immediately while the tofu is still warm.

OR YOU CAN TRY THIS...
– Use sliced Japanese daikon instead of radishes.
– Add some pickled chillies to the baguette.
– Try chopped Thai basil or mint instead of coriander.

TIP: Whizz the discarded soft bread in a food processor to make breadcrumbs.

SMOKED TOFU & BROCCOLI NOODLE JARS

SERVES: 4 | **PREP:** 15 MINUTES | **COOK:** 10-15 MINUTES

For the dressing:
4 tbsp peanut butter
1 garlic clove, crushed
2 tbsp light soy sauce
1 tbsp groundnut (peanut) oil
1 tbsp rice vinegar

For the salad:
225g/8oz rice vermicelli noodles
225g/8oz broccoli, cut into small florets
225g/8oz smoked tofu, cut into cubes
1 tbsp olive oil
175g/6oz frozen edamame (soy) beans, defrosted (see Tip)
½ small Chinese leaf (Chinese cabbage), shredded
sweet chilli sauce for drizzling (optional)

TIP: To defrost frozen edamame (soy) beans pour boiling water over and drain.

These salad jars can be prepared the night before for a tasty packed lunch. The secret of keeping the vegetables crunchy and fresh is to layer them in the correct order. The dressing goes first at the bottom of the jar, followed by noodles, pasta or grains, and then the firmer vegetables and protein in the middle, with crisp leafy greens and salad leaves on top.

1 Combine all the dressing ingredients in a small jug and whisk until smooth and creamy, adding a splash of water to mix, if necessary. Pour the dressing into 4 lidded glass jars (approximately 225g/8oz capacity).

2 Cook the noodles following the pack instructions. Drain well.

3 Steam the broccoli in a steamer basket or colander over a saucepan of simmering water for 3 minutes, or until just tender (not soft) and still bright green.

4 Pat the tofu dry with kitchen paper (paper towels). Heat the oil in a small non-stick frying pan (skillet) over a high heat and fry the tofu for 4–5 minutes, turning it occasionally, until golden brown all over. Remove from the pan and drain on kitchen paper.

5 Divide the cold noodles between the jars and then add a layer of edamame beans, followed by a layer of tofu and then broccoli. Top with the shredded Chinese leaves. Seal the jars and keep in a cool place until you're ready to eat.

6 Before serving, gently shake the jars to coat everything in the dressing or tip the contents into a bowl and stir. Serve drizzled with sweet chilli sauce, if you like.

OR YOU CAN TRY THIS...
– Add some beansprouts or other sprouting seeds.
– Add some diced red bird's eye chilli or crushed chilli flakes.

ROASTED SWEET POTATO & TOFU BOWLS WITH PESTO

SERVES: 4 | **PREP:** 15 MINUTES | **COOK:** 25-30 MINUTES

4 medium sweet potatoes, peeled and cut into wedges

1 large red onion, cut into wedges

4 tbsp olive oil, plus extra for brushing

4 sprigs of thyme

1 tbsp balsamic vinegar

400g/14oz extra-firm tofu, pressed (see page 10) and cut into cubes

150g/5oz fine green beans, trimmed

60g/2oz sun-blush tomatoes, drained and chopped

4 heaped tbsp green pesto

salt and freshly ground black pepper

Bowl food is so easy and great for casual meals and TV suppers. The quality of the pesto makes all the difference to this dish. If possible, use freshly made from the deli or supermarket rather than from a jar.

1 Preheat the oven to 190°C, 375°F, gas mark 5.

2 Toss the sweet potatoes and red onions in half the oil and place on a baking tray (cookie sheet). Strip the leaves from the sprigs of thyme and sprinkle over the top. Season lightly with salt and pepper,

3 Mix the remaining olive oil with the balsamic vinegar in a bowl. Add the tofu and stir gently to coat the cubes. Season with salt and pepper. Lightly brush a second baking tray with oil and add the tofu in a single layer.

4 Bake the sweet potatoes, red onions and tofu in the oven for 25–30 minutes until the vegetable are tender and the tofu is golden brown. Check the tofu after 20 minutes in case it is browning too fast.

5 Meanwhile, cook the green beans in a saucepan of boiling water for 3–4 minutes, until just tender. Drain well.

6 Divide the roasted vegetables and tofu between 4 shallow serving bowls. Sprinkle the sun-blush tomatoes over the tofu, then add the green beans to the bowls. Drizzle with the pesto and serve.

OR YOU CAN TRY THIS...

– Add some red or yellow (bell) peppers, cherry tomatoes or aubergine (eggplant).
– Add some garlic cloves, fennel, coriander or cumin seeds.
– Use red pesto instead of green.
– Substitute any green vegetables for the beans, e.g. broccoli, spinach, kale or courgettes (zucchini).

TOFU TOM YUM WITH NOODLES

SERVES: 4 | **PREP:** 10 MINUTES | **COOK:** 20 MINUTES

250g/9oz soba noodles

1.2 litres/2 pints (5 cups) vegetable stock (broth)

3 fresh or dried kaffir lime leaves

1 tbsp soft brown sugar

2 lemongrass stalks, bashed

2 red bird's eye chillies, thinly sliced

4 garlic cloves, thinly sliced

225g/8oz cherry or baby plum tomatoes, halved

4 spring onions (scallions), thinly sliced

2 tbsp soy sauce

2 tbsp vegan fish sauce or tamari

juice of 1 lime

2 pak choi (bok choy), sliced

225g/8oz firm tofu, cut into cubes

a handful of coriander (cilantro), chopped

Traditional tom yum soup is made with prawns (shrimp) but this aromatic vegetarian version with tofu is just as good. Quick and easy to make, it's perfect for a light meal or when you feel like something warming and fragrant.

1 Cook the noodles following the pack instructions. Drain and set aside.

2 Meanwhile, pour the vegetable stock into a large saucepan and bring to the boil. Reduce the heat and add the kaffir lime leaves, sugar, lemongrass, chillies and garlic. Simmer gently for 10 minutes.

3 Add the tomatoes and spring onions and simmer for 5 minutes. Stir in the soy sauce, fish sauce, lime juice and pak choi and cook for 2–3 minutes until the greens wilt but retain their 'bite'. Remove and discard the lemongrass and lime leaves.

4 Divide the cooked noodles between 4 serving bowls. Add the tofu and pour the soup over the top. Sprinkle with coriander and serve immediately.

OR YOU CAN TRY THIS...

– Add some freshly shaved coconut or thin matchsticks of fresh root ginger.
– Stir in some beansprouts at the end.
– Use rice noodles instead of soba noodles.
– Garnish with Thai basil or mint instead of coriander.

VIETNAMESE TOFU PHO

SERVES: 4 | **PREP:** 10 MINUTES | **COOK:** 1 HOUR 10 MINUTES

1 cinnamon stick
2 star anise
3 whole cloves
2 tsp coriander seeds, crushed
1 tsp fennel seeds
1 white onion, top and bottom trimmed
1.5 litres/2½ pints (6¼ cups) vegetable stock (broth)
2.5cm/1in piece fresh root ginger, peeled and diced
1 red bird's eye chilli, thinly sliced
2 tbsp vegan fish sauce or soy sauce
½ tsp sugar
300g/10oz rice noodles
2 tsp groundnut (peanut) oil
200g/7oz firm or extra-firm tofu, pressed (see page 10) and cut into cubes
1 bunch of spring onions (scallions), sliced diagonally
2 pak choi (bok choy), sliced
juice of 1 lime
a handful of coriander (cilantro), chopped
a handful of mint, chopped
soy sauce or hot chilli sauce, to serve

A whole hour might seem like a long time to simmer the broth but it really does make all the difference to the flavour of the finished soup. And you don't have to stand over it while it bubbles away – just prepare the vegetables and noodles and then chill and relax.

1 Place a non-stick frying pan (skillet) over a medium to high heat and when it's hot add the cinnamon stick, star anise, cloves and coriander and fennel seeds. Dry-roast the spices for 1–2 minutes, shaking the pan gently once or twice, until they release their aroma. Remove from the pan before they burn.

2 Put the whole onion on a very hot griddle pan over a high heat and cook each end until charred.

3 Pour the vegetable stock into a large saucepan and add the dry-roasted spices, charred onion, ginger, chilli, vegan fish sauce or soy sauce and sugar. Cover with a lid and simmer gently over a low heat for 1 hour.

4 Cook the rice noodles following the pack instructions and drain well.

5 Heat the oil in a large non-stick frying pan over a medium to high heat and fry the tofu for 4–5 minutes until crisp and golden brown all over. Remove and drain on kitchen paper (paper towels).

6 With a slotted spoon, remove the cinnamon stick, star anise and cloves from the hot broth. Add the spring onions, pak choi, lime juice and herbs. Cook for 1–2 minutes until the pak choi wilts.

7 Divide the noodles between 4 bowls and ladle the hot broth over the top. Add the fried tofu and serve with soy sauce or hot chilli sauce.

OR YOU CAN TRY THIS…

– Add some dried mushrooms to the simmering broth.
– Add an extra chilli or serve drizzled with Sriracha sauce.
– Flavour the broth with chopped fennel, carrot or celery.

INDIAN SPICED TOFU TANDOORI KEBABS

SERVES: 4 | **PREP:** 20 MINUTES | **MARINATE:** 1 HOUR | **COOK:** 7-10 MINUTES

For the raita:
115g/4oz (½ cup) dairy-free
    soya or coconut milk
    yoghurt alternative
¼ cucumber, diced
3 spring onions (scallions)
    diced
¼ tsp ground cumin
a handful of coriander
    (cilantro), chopped
salt and freshly ground
    black pepper

For the yoghurt marinade:
115g/4oz (½ cup) dairy-free
    soya or coconut milk
    yoghurt alternative
2 garlic cloves, crushed
1 tsp garam masala
1 tsp paprika
1 tsp ground turmeric
½ tsp chilli powder
a good pinch of salt

You can't beat the smoky aroma and flavour of chargrilled kebabs cooked outside over hot coals, but a large ridged griddle pan works nearly as well. The beauty of this dish is that you can make the marinade and cucumber raita in advance and then cook everything at the last minute.

1 Combine all the raita ingredients in a bowl and stir well. Cover and chill until you're ready to serve the kebabs.

2 Combine all the marinade ingredients in a bowl and stir will. Add the tofu and stir gently until the cubes are completely coated. Cover the bowl with clingfilm (plastic wrap) and chill in the fridge for at least 1 hour.

3 Meanwhile, soak 8 bamboo or wooden skewers in cold water to prevent them from burning during cooking.

4 Thread the marinated tofu, pepper chunks and red onion wedges alternately onto the skewers. Lightly brush a griddle pan with oil and set over a medium to high heat. Alternatively, oil the bars of a preheated barbecue.

For the kebabs:
400g/14oz extra-firm
   or firm tofu, pressed
   (see page 10) and cut
   into cubes
1 large red (bell) pepper,
   deseeded and cut into
   chunks
1 large green or yellow
   (bell) pepper, deseeded
   and cut into chunks
1 large red onion, cut into
   wedges
vegetable oil, for brushing
boiled rice, to serve

5 Cook the skewers for 7–10 minutes, turning occasionally, until the vegetables are tender and slightly charred and the tofu is attractively striped and golden. Cook the skewers in a couple of batches, if necessary. Serve the kebabs on a bed of boiled rice with the raita.

OR YOU CAN TRY THIS...
– Buy some ready-made tandoori paste and stir it into the yoghurt.
– Use courgettes (zucchini), fennel, mushrooms or cherry tomatoes instead of peppers.

TOFU CHILAQUILES

SERVES: 4 | **PREP:** 15 MINUTES | **COOK:** 20–25 MINUTES

For the spicy tomato sauce:
1 tbsp olive oil
1 red onion, chopped
2 garlic cloves, crushed
2 tsp chilli powder
1 tsp ground cumin
400g/14oz can chopped
   tomatoes
1 tbsp tomato purée (paste)
4 tbsp vegetable stock (broth)
salt and freshly ground
   black pepper

For the chilaquiles:
1 tbsp olive oil
2 garlic cloves, crushed
4 spring onions (scallions),
   thinly sliced
½ tsp ground cumin
½ tsp turmeric
a pinch of chilli powder
400g/14oz extra-firm or
   firm tofu, pressed
   (see page 10)
150g/5oz (4 cups) tortilla
   chips
a handful of coriander
   (cilantro), chopped
100g/3½oz (1 cup) grated
   Monterey Jack or vegan
   cheese-style block
1 ripe avocado, peeled,
   stoned (pitted) and sliced
lime wedges, to serve

Chilaquiles are eaten for breakfast in Mexico but they are also great for brunch. Be sure to add the tortilla chips to the spicy tomato sauce at the very last minute, so they stay quite crisp and don't go soggy.

1 To make the sauce, heat the oil in a non-stick frying pan (skillet) over a medium heat. Cook the onion and garlic, stirring occasionally, for 6–8 minutes until softened and golden. Stir in the spices and cook for 1 minute. Add the tomatoes, tomato purée and stock and turn up the heat. Cook for about 5 minutes until the sauce reduces and thickens slightly.

2 Season to taste with salt and pepper, then remove from the heat and pour the sauce into a blender or food processor. Blitz until smooth.

3 For the chilaquiles, heat the olive oil in a non-stick frying pan over a medium heat and cook the garlic and spring onions for 2–3 minutes without browning. Stir in the spices and cook for 1 minute. With your hands, crumble the tofu into the pan and stir gently until it's coated with spicy oil. Cook for about 5 minutes, adding a little water to keep it moist if it's too dry.

4 Just before you are ready to eat, stir three-quarters of the tortilla chips into the spicy tomato sauce. Divide between 4 shallow serving bowls and top with the tofu mixture. Sprinkle with the coriander and grated cheese and serve immediately with the remaining tortilla chips, avocado slices and lime wedges.

OR YOU CAN TRY THIS...

– Drizzle with dairy-free coconut milk yoghurt alternative or vegan cashew cream.
– Serve with black or refried beans, hot salsa, pico di gallo or guacamole.
– Instead of chilli powder use hot dried ancho chillies or fresh chipotle chillies.
– Sprinkle with diced red onion.

GRIDDLED TOFU & SPRING VEGETABLES WITH SALSA VERDE

SERVES: 4 | **PREP:** 15 MINUTES | **COOK:** 20-30 MINUTES

For the salsa verde:
2 garlic cloves
½ tsp coarse sea salt
1 bunch of flat-leaf parsley,
    chopped
a handful of tarragon,
    chopped
a handful of mint, chopped
2 tbsp capers, chopped
1 tbsp Dijon or tarragon
    mustard
juice of ½ lemon
2 tbsp red wine vinegar
120ml/4fl oz (½ cup) fruity
    green olive oil

For the tofu and vegetables:
225g/8oz (1 cup) brown rice
400g/14oz extra-firm
    or firm tofu, pressed
    (see page 10)
2 tbsp olive oil, plus extra
    for brushing
grated zest of 1 lemon
300g/10oz asparagus,
    trimmed
1 fennel bulb, trimmed
    and cut into wedges
1 bunch of spring onions
    (scallions), trimmed
salt and freshly ground
    black pepper

This fresh-tasting combo of spring vegetables and tofu in a lovely piquant green sauce is perfect for a healthy light meal. If you don't want to make the salsa verde you could cheat and just drizzle some green pesto over the tofu.

1 Cook the rice following the pack instructions.

2 For the salsa verde, crush the garlic and salt together and add to a bowl with the herbs, capers and mustard. Stir in the lemon juice and vinegar, then gradually drizzle in the olive oil until you have a thick sauce.

3 Cut the tofu into 4 thick slices. Combine 1 tablespoon olive oil with the lemon zest and some salt and pepper and brush it over both sides of the tofu.

4 Place a non-stick griddle pan over a medium to high heat and cook the tofu for 3–4 minutes, or until crisp and golden brown. Turn it over and cook the other side. Remove, drain on kitchen paper (paper towels) and keep warm.

5 Add the remaining oil to the pan and cook the asparagus, fennel and spring onions (in batches), turning occasionally, for about 5 minutes until tender and slightly charred.

6 Arrange the tofu and griddled vegetables on 4 serving plates and spoon the salsa verde over the top. Serve immediately with the brown rice.

OR YOU CAN TRY THIS...
– Serve with quinoa instead of rice.
– Add some chilli or garlic powder to the tofu marinade.
– Add other green vegetables, such as courgettes (zucchini), green beans or mangetout (snow peas).

CRISPY CHINESE-STYLE TOFU PANCAKES

SERVES: 4 | **PREP:** 15 MINUTES | **COOK:** 5 MINUTES

400g/14oz extra-firm tofu, pressed (see page 10) and cut into thin slices
2 tbsp sesame oil
1 tbsp Chinese five spice powder
100g/3½oz (scant ½ cup) hoisin sauce
16 thin Chinese pancakes
1 bunch of spring onions (scallions), shredded
½ cucumber, cut into thin matchsticks
a handful of coriander (cilantro), chopped
2 red chillies, deseeded and shredded
white sesame seeds, for sprinkling

We are all familiar with shredded crispy duck but how about this vegan recipe using tofu instead? You can buy packs of thin Chinese pancakes in many large supermarket chains as well as Asian supermarkets and delis.

1 Cut the pressed tofu into thin slices. Mix half the sesame oil with the five spice powder and 1 tablespoon of the hoisin sauce in a bowl. Add the tofu and gently turn in the mixture until lightly coated.

2 Heat the remaining sesame oil in a non-stick frying pan (skillet) over a medium to high heat. When the oil is hot, add the tofu and cook, turning once or twice, for 2–4 minutes until crisp and browned. Remove and drain on kitchen paper (paper towels).

3 Meanwhile, steam the pancakes, in a bamboo steamer or a colander lined with foil suspended over a pan of simmering water, for 1–2 minutes. Keep warm.

4 To serve, put everything on the table and let people assemble their own pancakes. Spread a little hoisin sauce over each warm pancake and top with some spring onions, cucumber and crispy tofu. Sprinkle with a little coriander and chilli and some sesame seeds and roll up tightly.

TIP: You can also heat the pancakes in a microwave. Just follow the instructions on the packet.

TOFU BREAKFAST SCRAMBLE

SERVES: 4 | **PREP:** 10 MINUTES | **COOK:** 15 MINUTES

2 tbsp olive oil
300g/10oz mushrooms,
    sliced
16 cherry tomatoes, halved
400g/14oz spinach,
    trimmed
1 tsp turmeric
½ tsp ground cumin
½ tsp smoked paprika
a good pinch of garlic
    powder
400g/14oz extra-firm
    or firm tofu, pressed
    (see page 10)
1 tsp soy sauce or tamari
1 small bunch of chives,
    snipped
salt and freshly ground black
    pepper
Sriracha or sweet chilli
    sauce, for drizzling
wholemeal or wholegrain
    toast, to serve

This is a delicious and healthy way to kick-start your day. And it's highly nutritious, too, providing not only high-quality protein but also contributing to your five-a-day portions of fruit and vegetables.

1 Heat half the olive oil in a large non-stick frying pan (skillet) over a medium heat. Cook the mushrooms, turning occasionally, for 3–4 minutes until golden. Add the tomatoes and spinach and cook for 3–4 minutes until the spinach wilts and softens slightly. Season to taste with salt and pepper.

2 Heat the remaining oil in another pan over a medium to high heat and stir in the spices and garlic powder. With your hands, crumble the tofu into the pan, add the soy sauce and stir gently. Cook for about 5 minutes, adding a little water or more soy sauce to keep it moist if it's too dry.

3 Divide the vegetables between 4 serving plates or shallow bowls. Spoon the tofu over the top and sprinkle with the chives. Drizzle with Sriracha or sweet chilli sauce and serve immediately with hot toast.

OR YOU CAN TRY THIS...

– Sprinkle with sunflower, pumpkin or fennel seeds.
– Add some chopped spring onions (scallions), asparagus, courgettes (zucchini) or red (bell) peppers.
– Use kale instead of spinach.
– Sprinkle with lemon juice.

TOFU SHAWARMA

SERVES: 4 | **PREP:** 15 MINUTES | **MARINATE:** 1 HOUR | **COOK:** 10-15 MINUTES

For the shawarma marinade:
115g/4oz (½ cup) 0% fat
    Greek yoghurt or dairy-
    free yoghurt alternative
juice of 1 lemon
3 garlic cloves, crushed
1 tsp fennel seeds
1 tsp grated fresh root
    ginger
1 tsp ground cumin
1 tsp paprika
a pinch of ground nutmeg
¼ tsp dried oregano
a good pinch of salt

For the filling:
450g/1lb extra-firm or
    firm tofu, pressed
    (see page 10)
4 large pitta breads
shredded lettuce and sliced
    tomatoes, to serve
pickled cucumbers or
    pickled hot chillies,
    to serve
4 tbsp hummus
1–2 tsp harissa
salt and freshly ground
    black pepper

Spicy, aromatic shawarma is usually made with meat and is popular throughout the Levant. This marinated tofu version is a great vegetarian alternative. It's usually served in pitta or flatbreads with hot pickles and pungent garlic sauce but we've used hummus and a dash of fiery red harissa instead.

1 Mix together all the ingredients for the shawarma marinade in a shallow dish.

2 Cut the tofu into slices and add to the marinade, turning it gently until coated. Cover and chill in the fridge for at least 1 hour.

3 Preheat the oven to 200°C, 400°F, gas mark 6. Line a baking tray (cookie sheet) with foil.

4 Arrange the tofu in a single layer on the lined tray. Bake in the oven for 20–30 minutes until golden brown.

5 Warm the pitta breads in a lightly oiled griddle pan or frying pan (skillet). Cut them open down one side with a sharp knife.

6 Divide the hot tofu between the split pitta breads, stuffing it into the middle with some lettuce, tomatoes and the pickled cucumbers or chillies. Add the hummus and a dash of harissa and serve immediately.

OR YOU CAN TRY THIS...
– Roll up the tofu shawarma, salad and pickles in some large warm wraps.
– Use griddled flatbreads instead of pitta.
– Add some diced feta or a little tahini.

GRIDDLED TOFU GYROS

SERVES: 4 | **PREP:** 15 MINUTES | **COOK:** 20 MINUTES

For the tzatziki:
225g/8oz (1 cup) dairy-free
    soya or coconut milk
    yoghurt alternative
1 tbsp olive oil
½ cucumber, diced
2 garlic cloves, crushed
a few sprigs of mint, finely
    chopped
a few sprigs of dill, finely
    chopped
grated zest and juice of
    ½ lemon
salt and freshly ground
    black pepper

For the gyros:
2 aubergines (eggplants),
    thickly sliced
olive oil, for brushing
1 tsp za'atar
1 tsp dried oregano or
    marjoram
400g/14oz extra-firm or firm
    tofu, pressed (see page 10)
    and cut into strips
4 large flatbreads or thick
    pitta breads
¼ cucumber, sliced
4 tomatoes, quartered
½ red onion, thinly sliced
crisp lettuce leaves, shredded
1–2 tsp harissa
lemon wedges, to serve

Gyros are traditional Greek street food made with meat, especially pork or chicken, then wrapped up with salad and fried potatoes in a thick, soft flatbread and drizzled with garlic sauce. But you can make this wonderful vegan version with tofu and aubergines.

1 For the tzatziki, combine all the ingredients together in a bowl and stir well. Season to taste with salt and pepper.

2 Brush the aubergine slices on both sides with oil. Sprinkle with the za'atar and herbs and season lightly with salt and pepper.

3 Place a large griddle pan over a medium to high heat and, when it's hot, add some aubergine slices (do this in batches). Cook for 2–3 minutes each side, or until charred, golden brown and attractively striped. Drain on kitchen paper (paper towels) and keep warm.

4 Season the tofu with salt and pepper and brush some more oil over the hot griddle pan. Cook the tofu for about 5 minutes, turning until browned and golden all over. Remove and drain on kitchen paper.

5 Warm the flatbreads or pitta breads in a lightly oiled griddle pan or frying pan (skillet). Divide the griddled aubergines and tofu, cucumber, tomatoes, onion and lettuce between them. Season lightly with salt and pepper and drizzle with tzatziki. Add a dash of harissa.

6 Place each flatbread on a square of foil or baking parchment and fold up or roll over to enclose the filling. Eat immediately, with a squeeze of lemon, while they are warm.

OR YOU CAN TRY THIS...

– Use hummus or tahini sauce instead of tzatziki.
– Drizzle with hot chilli sauce.

SWEET & SOUR CHILLI TOFU

SERVES: 4 | **PREP:** 15 MINUTES | **COOK:** 30-35 MINUTES

400g/14oz extra-firm
or firm tofu, pressed
(see page 10)
3 tbsp cornflour (cornstarch)
vegetable oil, for frying
1 onion, finely chopped
1 tsp black mustard seeds
1 tsp cumin seeds
1 tsp coriander seeds,
crushed
2.5cm/1in piece fresh root
ginger, peeled and diced
2 garlic cloves, crushed
1 tbsp tomato purée (paste)
3 tbsp sweet chilli sauce
2 tbsp soy sauce or tamari
2 tsp soft brown sugar
120ml/4fl oz (½ cup)
vegetable stock (broth)
500g/1lb 2oz spinach,
trimmed
salt and freshly ground
black pepper
boiled rice and cucumber
raita (see page 38),
to serve

Chunks of tofu in a sweet and sour chilli sauce make a delicious lunch or light supper. You can prepare the sauce in advance to reheat later.

1 Cut the tofu into cubes and turn it gently in the cornflour until lightly coated. Season with salt and pepper.

2 Pour 5mm/¼in oil into a large non-stick frying pan (skillet) and set over a medium heat. When the oil is hot, add the tofu (in batches) and cook, turning occasionally, for 3–4 minutes until crisp and golden brown. Remove and drain on kitchen paper (paper towels). Transfer the remaining oil to a heatproof jug.

3 Heat 1 tablespoon of the reserved oil in the frying pan over a low heat. Cook the onion, stirring occasionally, for 8–10 minutes until really tender. Add the seeds, ginger and garlic and cook for 4–5 minutes.

4 Stir in the tomato purée, sweet chilli sauce, soy sauce or tamari and sugar and cook for 1 minute. Turn up the heat to medium and add the vegetable stock. Let the mixture bubble away for about 5 minutes until it reduces and thickens slightly. Season to taste with salt or more sweet chilli or soy sauce, depending on how sweet or salty you like it.

5 Meanwhile, cook the spinach with 1 tablespoon water in a large saucepan, covered with a lid and set over a medium heat, shaking the pan occasionally, for about 2 minutes, or until the spinach wilts and turns a lovely bright green. Drain in a colander, pressing down with the back of a spoon to release all the moisture.

6 Stir the fried tofu into the spicy sauce and warm through gently. Serve immediately with the spinach and some boiled rice and cucumber raita.

OR YOU CAN TRY THIS...
– Add some sliced aubergine (eggplant), red (bell) peppers or green beans.
– For a sweeter sauce, add 1 teaspoon caster (superfine) sugar.
– For a hotter sauce, add a diced chilli.
– Substitute kale for spinach.
– Serve with yoghurt instead of raita and some poppadums or chapatis.

MARINATED TOFU STEAKS WITH THAI SALSA

SERVES: 4 | **PREP:** 20 MINUTES | **MARINATE:** 1 HOUR | **COOK:** 6-16 MINUTES

For the tofu steaks:
600g/1lb 5oz extra-firm
    or firm tofu, pressed
    (see page 10)
juice of 2 limes
3 tbsp soy sauce
2 tbsp vegetable oil, e.g.
    toasted sesame, sunflower
    or rapeseed
freshly ground black pepper

For the Thai salsa:
4 ripe tomatoes, diced
4 spring onions (scallions),
    chopped
1 lemongrass stalk, peeled
    and diced
1 red bird's eye chilli, diced
1 garlic clove, crushed
1 tbsp grated fresh root
    ginger
a handful of coriander
    (cilantro), chopped
a few sprigs of mint,
    chopped
juice of 1 lime, plus extra
    to taste
2 tsp nam pla (Thai fish
    sauce), plus extra to taste
1 tsp palm sugar, plus extra
    to taste
boiled rice or rice noodles,
    to serve

If you don't have a griddle pan, you can cook the tofu steaks under a grill (broiler) or over hot coals on a barbecue. Vegetarians can use vegan 'fish' sauce instead of nam pla in the salsa.

1 Cut the tofu into 8 thick slices and place in a shallow bowl. Combine the lime juice, soy sauce and 1 tablespoon oil and then pour over the tofu. Turn it in the marinade and add a grinding of black pepper. Cover and chill in the fridge for at least 1 hour.

2 Combine all the Thai salsa ingredients together in a bowl and stir well. Taste and add more lime juice, nam pla or sugar, if needed.

3 Brush a non-stick griddle pan with the remaining oil and place over a medium to high heat. When it's hot, carefully add the marinated tofu (you may have to do this in two batches) and cook for 3–4 minutes, or until crisping and golden brown. Turn it over and cook the other side. Remove and drain on kitchen paper (paper towels).

4 Serve the tofu immediately with boiled rice or noodles and the Thai salsa on the side.

OR YOU CAN TRY THIS...
– Add some diced cucumber or Thai basil to the salsa.
– Drizzle with some sweet chilli sauce.

DAIRY-FREE TOFU QUICHE

SERVES: 6 | **PREP:** 25 MINUTES | **COOK:** 1 HOUR

3 tbsp olive oil, plus extra
  for brushing
2 leeks, trimmed and
  thickly sliced
2 garlic cloves, crushed
300g/10oz white or
  chestnut mushrooms,
  thickly sliced
175g/6oz cherry tomatoes,
  halved
400g/14oz baby spinach
250g/9oz filo (phyllo) pastry
400g/14oz silken tofu
2 tbsp nutritional yeast
1 bunch of chives, snipped
salt and freshly ground
  black pepper

TIPS

– If the filling is too thick
  stir in some nut milk
  alternative. If it's too thick
  it won't have a creamy
  consistency.

– This quiche keeps well in
  the fridge for up to 2 days
  and can be reheated in
  the oven at 200°C, 400°F,
  gas mark 6 until warmed
  through.

This is the perfect tart if you're a vegetarian or vegan. It's made without eggs or dairy products and the delicious vegetable and tofu filling is encased in crisp filo pastry.

1 Preheat the oven to 200°C, 400°F, gas mark 6.

2 Heat the oil in a large non-stick frying pan (skillet) set over a low to medium heat. Cook the leeks and garlic for about 10 minutes until tender and golden. Remove from the pan and set aside.

3 Add the mushrooms to the pan and cook, stirring occasionally, for 5 minutes, or until golden brown. Stir in the tomatoes and spinach and cook for 2–3 minutes until the spinach wilts and the tomatoes are just tender. Return the leeks to the pan and season with salt and pepper.

4 Meanwhile, brush a 25cm/10in round loose-bottomed flan tin (pie pan with removable bottom) with olive oil. Remove the filo sheets from the pack and cover them with a damp cloth to prevent them drying out while you assemble the quiche. Lightly brush 1 sheet with oil and use to line the tin, letting any leftover pastry overlap the edges. Repeat with all the pastry sheets, brushing each one with oil, until they are all used up. Using your hands, scrunch up the pastry edges, folding them inwards to make an outside crust for the tart. Prick the base with a fork.

5 Bake in the oven for 10 minutes until crisp and golden. Remove from the oven and reduce the temperature to 190°C, 375°F, gas mark 5.

6 Put the tofu and nutritional yeast in a food processor and blend until smooth and creamy. Transfer to a large bowl and gently mix in the cooked vegetables and chives.

7 Spoon the tofu and vegetable mixture into the centre of the filo crust and level the filling with the back of a spoon. Bake in the oven for about 30 minutes, or until the filling is set, firm and golden brown. Cover the edges of the pastry with foil if they start to brown too much.

8 Serve warm, cut into wedges.

TOFU TRICOLORE SALAD

SERVES: 4 | **PREP:** 10 MINUTES

For the dressing:
1 tbsp olive oil
1 tbsp soy sauce
1 tbsp balsamic vinegar
juice of 1 lime
1 tbsp clear honey or
    maple syrup

For the salad:
400g/14oz large ripe
    tomatoes, thinly sliced
1 ripe avocado, peeled,
    stoned (pitted) and
    thinly sliced
400g/14oz block silken
    tofu, sliced
4 spring onions (scallions),
    thinly sliced
a few basil leaves
freshly ground black
    pepper

In this twist on a classic tricolore salad with mozzarella, we've used moist silken tofu instead. For a caprese salad, omit the avocado. You can use any basil, including the familiar Mediterranean variety, the smaller leafed Greek basil or Thai basil.

1 Combine all the dressing ingredients in a bowl and whisk well.

2 Arrange the tomato, avocado and tofu slices in attractive overlapping rows or concentric circles. Grind some black pepper over the top.

3 Sprinkle with the spring onions and dressing. Scatter the basil leaves over the top and serve immediately.

OR YOU CAN TRY THIS...
– Use mint or coriander (cilantro) instead of basil.
– Add some wild rocket (arugula) or baby spinach.
– Use sweet cherry or baby plum tomatoes.

STIR-FRIED NOODLE SALAD WITH BROCCOLI & TOFU

SERVES: 4 | **PREP:** 10 MINUTES | **COOK:** 15 MINUTES

For the dressing:
4 tbsp tamari or soy sauce
2 tbsp rice vinegar
1 tsp sesame oil
a good pinch of sugar

For the salad:
225g/8oz egg noodles
1 tbsp vegetable oil
1 large carrot, cut into thin matchsticks
1 red (bell) pepper, deseeded and thinly sliced
2 garlic cloves, crushed
2 red bird's eye chillies, shredded
2.5cm/1in piece fresh root ginger, peeled and diced
400g/14oz firm or extra-firm tofu, pressed (see page 10) and cut into cubes
450g/1lb Tenderstem® or purple-sprouting broccoli, trimmed
4 spring onions (scallions), shredded
a handful of coriander (cilantro), chopped

This warm substantial salad is easy to make and quick to cook. You can stir-fry the broccoli instead of steaming it but it will lose its lovely fresh green colour and it won't be as tender.

1 Combine all the dressing ingredients together in a small bowl and stir well.

2 Cook the noodles following the pack instructions. Drain well.

3 Heat the oil in a large non-stick wok or frying pan (skillet) set over a medium to high heat and stir-fry the carrot and red pepper for 3 minutes. Add the garlic, chillies and ginger and cook for 2 minutes. Add the tofu and stir-fry for 2–3 minutes.

4 Meanwhile, steam the broccoli in a steamer basket or colander over a saucepan of boiling water for 3–4 minutes until it is just tender but still retains some bite.

5 Add the noodles and broccoli to the wok and toss gently in the dressing. Divide between 4 serving plates or shallow bowls and sprinkle with the spring onions and coriander. Serve warm.

OR YOU CAN TRY THIS...
– Use small broccoli florets from a head of calabrese.
– Add any vegetables you fancy to the stir-fry: beansprouts, shredded cabbage, courgettes (zucchini) or pak choi (bok choy).
– Use rice noodles instead of egg noodles.

VIETNAMESE TOFU SALAD

SERVES: 4 | **PREP:** 20 MINUTES | **SOAKING:** 12-15 MINUTES | **COOK:** 4 MINUTES

For the dressing:
1 red bird's eye chilli, chopped
1 garlic clove, thinly sliced
2 tbsp nam pla (Thai fish sauce)
1 tbsp rice vinegar
juice of 1 lime
1 tsp caster (superfine) sugar

For the salad:
200g/7oz rice noodles
60g/2oz (scant ½ cup)
    unsalted peanuts
2 carrots, peeled into long
    thin strips
1 large courgette (zucchini),
    peeled into long thin strips
100g/3½oz mangetout
    (snow peas), trimmed and
    halved lengthways
1 bunch of spring onions
    (scallions), thinly sliced
½ cucumber, cut into strips
2 little gem lettuces, trimmed
    and separated into leaves
400g/14oz extra-firm tofu,
    pressed (see page 10) and
    cut into cubes
1 tbsp soy sauce
1 tbsp sweet chilli sauce
1 tbsp vegetable oil
a few basil leaves, chopped
a handful of coriander
    (cilantro), chopped
lime wedges, to serve

A really fresh-tasting salad that's hearty enough to enjoy as a main meal. Vegetarians and vegans can substitute soy sauce or tamari for the nam pla in the dressing. The thinner the strips of carrot, courgette and cucumber, the better – you don't need a spiralizer; a vegetable peeler works just as well.

1 Add all the dressing ingredients to a bowl and whisk to combine.

2 Soak the rice noodles in plenty of cold water for 12–15 minutes, or until softened (or follow the instructions on the pack). Drain well.

3 Place a non-stick frying pan (skillet) over a medium to high heat. When it's hot, add the peanuts and toss gently until they are golden brown and fragrant. Remove immediately, before they burn, and chop them coarsely.

4 Mix together the carrots, courgette, mangetout, spring onions, cucumber and lettuce in a large bowl.

5 Place the tofu cubes in a bowl with the soy sauce and sweet chilli sauce. Stir together gently to lightly coat the tofu. Heat the oil in a non-stick frying pan set over a medium to high heat, and when it's hot add the tofu. Cook for about 4 minutes, turning, until golden brown all over. Remove and drain on kitchen paper (paper towels).

6 Stir the drained rice noodles into the vegetables and toss lightly in the dressing. Divide between 4 serving plates and top with the hot tofu. Sprinkle with the chopped herbs and toasted peanuts. Serve immediately with lime wedges.

OR YOU CAN TRY THIS...
– Omit the noodles and serve with boiled rice.
– Add some thinly sliced red or yellow (bell) peppers or beansprouts.
– Use mint instead of basil or coriander.

TOFU & EDAMAME BEAN SALAD

SERVES: 4 | **PREP:** 15 MINUTES | **COOK:** 15 MINUTES

For the dressing:
1cm/½in piece fresh root
  ginger, peeled and grated
1 red bird's eye chilli,
  deseeded and shredded
1 garlic clove, crushed
2 tbsp toasted sesame oil
1 tbsp tamari
juice of 1 orange

For the salad:
200g/7oz soba noodles
300g/10oz (2 cups) fresh
  or frozen edamame
  (soy) beans
225g/8oz (2 cups)
  beansprouts
100g/3½oz baby spinach
½ cucumber, cut into
  matchsticks
4 spring onions (scallions),
  thinly sliced
1 ripe avocado, peeled,
  stoned (pitted) and
  thinly sliced
250g/9oz firm or extra-
  firm tofu, pressed
  (see page 10)
1 tbsp vegetable oil
a small handful of coriander
  (cilantro), chopped
salt and freshly ground
  black pepper

This healthy green salad is surprisingly filling and packed with protein from the edamame beans and tofu. You can prepare the dressing, noodles and beans a few hours in advance and then assemble the salad and cook the tofu just before you're ready to eat.

1 Combine all the dressing ingredients in a bowl and whisk together.

2 Cook the noodles following the pack instructions. Drain and refresh under cold running water. Drain well.

3 Meanwhile, cook the edamame beans in a saucepan of boiling water for 2 minutes. Drain and refresh under cold running water. Drain well.

4 Mix together the beansprouts, spinach, cucumber, spring onions and avocado in a large bowl. Add the drained noodles and edamame beans and toss together.

5 Cut the tofu into 8 slices and season generously with salt and pepper. Heat the oil in a griddle pan set over a medium to high heat. When the pan is hot, add the tofu and cook for 2–3 minutes until golden and striped underneath. Carefully turn the tofu over and cook the other side.

6 Divide the salad between 4 serving plates or shallow bowls. Top with the griddled tofu and sprinkle with coriander. Serve immediately while the tofu is hot.

OR YOU CAN TRY THIS...

– Marinate the tofu in some soy sauce and garlic before griddling.
– Use rice or egg noodles.
– Add some broccoli florets or pak choi (bok choy) to the salad.
– For a sharper dressing, use lemon or lime juice.

CRISPY TOFU SALAD

SERVES: 4 | **PREP:** 15 MINUTES | **COOK:** 5 MINUTES

~~~~~~~~~~~~~~~~~~~~~

For the sesame seed dressing:

2 tbsp tahini

2 tbsp light soy sauce

2 tbsp rice vinegar

1 tbsp sesame oil

1 tsp agave syrup or clear honey

2 tbsp black sesame seeds

For the salad:

60g/2oz (scant ½ cup) cashews

2 large carrots, cut into thin matchsticks

200g/7oz Chinese leaf (Chinese cabbage), trimmed and shredded

1 bunch of radishes, trimmed and sliced

1 bunch of spring onions (scallions), thinly sliced

100g/3½oz baby spinach

85g/3oz (1 cup) alfalfa sprouted seeds or beansprouts

400g/14oz firm or extra-firm tofu, pressed (see page 10)

1 tbsp sesame oil

salt and freshly ground black pepper

Crisply fried tofu, crunchy salad vegetables and a sesame dressing make a winning combo. This salad is so healthy and wholesome – it makes a great speedy midweek supper.

1 Combine all the dressing ingredients in a small bowl and whisk together. If it's too thick for your liking, thin it with a little water.

2 Place a non-stick frying pan (skillet) over a medium to high heat. When it's hot, add the cashews and toss gently until they are golden brown and fragrant. Remove immediately, before they burn, and chop them coarsely.

3 Mix the carrots, Chinese leaf, radishes, spring onions, spinach and alfalfa in a large bowl.

4 Cut the tofu into bite-sized cubes and season with salt and pepper Heat the sesame oil in a large non-stick frying pan over a medium to high heat. When the oil is very hot, add the tofu and cook for 4–5 minutes, turning once or twice, until golden brown all over. Remove and drain on kitchen paper (paper towels).

5 Toss the salad in most of the dressing and divide between 4 serving plates. Top with the tofu and toasted cashews and drizzle with the remaining dressing. Serve immediately while the tofu is hot.

OR YOU CAN TRY THIS...

– You can use any sprouted seeds, including amaranth, broccoli, radish, peas or beansprouts.

– Use toasted sesame oil instead of plain.

– Substitute walnuts, hazelnuts or pistachios for the cashews.

~~~~~~~~~~~~~~~~~~~~~

HERBY POTATO SALAD WITH TOFU MAYO

SERVES: 4 | **PREP:** 20 MINUTES | **COOK:** 15 MINUTES

For the salad:
900g/2lb small new
   potatoes, halved
2 bunches of spring onions
   (scallions), chopped
1 bunch of chives, snipped,
   plus extra for sprinkling
a handful of flat-leaf parsley,
   finely chopped
a handful of mint, finely
   chopped

For the tofu mayo:
225g/8oz silken tofu
grated zest and juice of
   ½ small lemon
2 tbsp cider apple vinegar
4 tbsp extra virgin olive oil
1 garlic clove, crushed
salt and freshly ground
   black pepper

For the best results, make this egg-free vegan mayo with some good-quality fruity extra virgin olive oil. If the oil is too light the mayo will be bland and lack flavour. Why not make some extra mayo and use it in sandwiches or with French fries? It will keep well in the fridge for up to a week.

1 Place the halved potatoes into a large saucepan, cover with plenty of cold water and bring to the boil. Boil for about 15 minutes until the potatoes are tender but not mushy. Drain well.

2 Meanwhile for the mayo, place the tofu, lemon zest and juice and vinegar in a blender and blitz. With the motor running, add the olive oil through the feed tube, in a steady stream, until the mixture is well combined and creamy. Stir in the garlic and season to taste with salt and pepper.

3 Drain the potatoes and if they are larger than bite-sized cut in half again. Place in a bowl with the spring onions, herbs and mayo. Toss the potatoes gently in the mayo while they are still warm. Sprinkle with snipped chives and serve warm or cold.

OR YOU CAN TRY THIS...
– Use chopped dill instead of mint.
– Use chopped red onion instead of spring onions.
– Add some chopped celery or fennel bulb.
– Add some dried or fresh herbs to the mayo, e.g. tarragon or dill.
– For a more piquant mayo, add some Dijon mustard or mustard powder.
– Use peanut (groundnut) oil instead of olive oil.

THAI-STYLE COLESLAW WITH MARINATED TOFU

SERVES: 4 | **PREP:** 15 MINUTES | **COOK:** 5-7 MINUTES

For the Thai dressing:
4 tbsp rice vinegar
1 tbsp sugar
2 tbsp soy sauce or nam pla
   (Thai fish sauce)
1 tbsp olive oil
1 tsp sesame oil
a dash of lime juice

For the salad:
200g/7oz Chinese leaf
   (Chinese cabbage) or
   white cabbage, shredded
2 pak choi (bok choy),
   thinly sliced
2 carrots, cut into thin
   matchsticks
100g/3½oz (1 cup)
   beansprouts
1 red (bell) pepper, deseeded
   and thinly sliced
6 spring onions (scallions),
   diagonally sliced
1 red bird's eye chilli,
   shredded
225g/8oz marinated tofu,
   cut into cubes
60g/2oz (scant ½ cup)
   roasted peanuts
a handful of coriander
   (cilantro), chopped

This flavour-packed coleslaw is mixed with ready-marinated tofu – it's available in blocks in health food stores and many supermarkets and is a great standby if you don't have time to do it yourself. It is usually flavoured with soy, teriyaki or tamari sauces and ginger, garlic or spices, and can be eaten straight from the pack or added to salads, stir-fries and other dishes.

1 For the dressing, heat the vinegar and sugar in a saucepan over a low heat, stirring until the sugar dissolves. Simmer for 3–5 minutes until slightly reduced and then remove from the heat. Leave to cool and then stir in the remaining ingredients.

2 Put the Chinese leaf, pak choi, carrots, beansprouts, red pepper, spring onions and chilli in a large bowl and mix together well. Add the tofu and gently toss in the dressing. Sprinkle with the peanuts and coriander and serve.

OR YOU CAN TRY THIS...

– Add some shredded spring greens or kale.
– Use chopped or grated red onion instead of spring onions.
– Add some grated apple or chopped mango or papaya (pawpaw).

CREAMY TOFU SALAD DRESSING

MAKES: 330ML/11FL OZ (GENEROUS 1¼ CUPS) | **PREP:** 10 MINUTES

225g/8oz silken tofu
2 garlic cloves, crushed
2 tbsp dried herbs, e.g. dill,
    parsley or mixed herbs
    or a handful of fresh
    chives and flat-leaf
    parsley, chopped
2 tsp Dijon mustard
2 tbsp cider apple vinegar
2 tbsp olive oil
3 tbsp agave syrup
salt and freshly ground
    black pepper

This creamy dressing is perfect for a vegan Caesar salad (without the eggs and anchovies), as well as pasta and potato salads. Or toss with crisp green salad leaves in the style of a ranch dressing.

1 Put all the ingredients in a blender and blitz until smooth. If the dressing is too thick for your liking, you can thin it with some cold water.

2 Taste the dressing and add more salt and pepper, mustard or agave if it's not salty, spicy or sweet enough for your taste. If you're not using it immediately, store in an airtight container in the fridge for up to 3 days.

OR YOU CAN TRY THIS...
– Use clear honey instead of agave as a sweetener.
– Substitute white wine vinegar for cider vinegar or use some lemon juice.
– Use garlic powder instead of fresh garlic.
– Add a good pinch of onion powder or grated lemon zest for extra flavour.
– A tablespoon of drained capers will add piquancy.

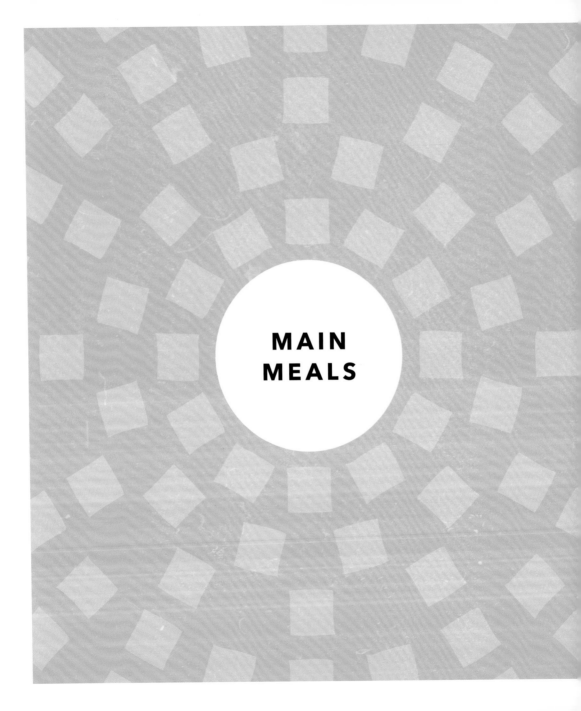

**MAIN
MEALS**

TOFU PAD THAI

SERVES: 4 | **PREP:** 15 MINUTES | **COOK:** 10 MINUTES

*For the cashew nut
  butter sauce:*
5 tbsp cashew nut butter
3 tbsp soy sauce
1 tbsp nam pla (Thai fish
  sauce) or vegan fish sauce
2 tbsp palm sugar
2 tbsp tamarind paste
grated zest and juice of
  2 limes

For the pad thai:
250g/9oz flat rice noodles
2 tbsp groundnut (peanut) oil
3 garlic cloves, crushed
2.5cm/1in piece fresh root
  ginger, peeled and diced
8 spring onions (scallions),
  sliced
1 red bird's eye chilli, diced
400g/14oz extra-firm
  or firm tofu, pressed
  (see page 10) and cut
  into cubes
100g/3½oz (1 cup)
  beansprouts
3 tbsp roasted cashews,
  crushed
2 tbsp sesame seeds
a handful of coriander
  (cilantro), chopped
lime wedges and sweet
  chilli sauce, to serve

If you've never considered using tofu in a pad thai, think again. Its subtle taste is the perfect foil for all the spicy, hot, salty and zingy flavours of the chilli, tamarind paste, lime and soy and fish sauces. This fabulous one-pan supper can be served in bowls and is so quick and easy to make… and there's minimal washing up.

1 Combine all the ingredients for the cashew nut butter sauce in a bowl and stir together with 2–3 tablespoons cold water.

2 Cook the rice noodles following the pack instructions. Drain.

3 Heat the oil in a non-stick wok or deep frying pan (skillet) set over a medium to high heat. Add the garlic, ginger, spring onions and chilli and stir-fry briskly for 1 minute. Add the tofu and cook for 5 minutes, turning several times, until golden all over. Stir in the cashew nut butter sauce, then reduce the heat, cover the pan and cook for 2 minutes.

4 Add the rice noodles and beansprouts and stir them gently into the sauce. Stir-fry for 1 minute, tossing them lightly.

5 Divide the mixture between 4 shallow serving bowls. Sprinkle with the roasted cashews, sesame seeds and coriander. Serve hot with lime wedges for squeezing and some sweet chilli sauce.

OR YOU CAN TRY THIS…
– Add some thin green beans or broccoli florets.
– Instead of cashew butter and roasted cashews, use peanut butter and roasted peanuts.
– Sprinkle with chopped basil or mint.
– Thin rice noodles can be used instead of the thicker flatter ones.

CHICKPEA, TOFU & SPINACH CURRY

SERVES: 4 | **PREP:** 10 MINUTES | **COOK:** 20-25 MINUTES

2 tbsp groundnut
 (peanut) oil
1 large onion, finely
 chopped
1 red (bell) pepper,
 deseeded and thinly
 sliced
2 garlic cloves, crushed
2.5cm/1in piece fresh root
 ginger, peeled and diced
1–2 tbsp curry paste
1 tsp ground turmeric
240ml/8fl oz (1 cup)
 coconut milk
120ml/4fl oz (½ cup)
 vegetable stock (broth)
60g/2oz (¼ cup) smooth
 peanut butter
400g/14oz extra-firm
 or firm tofu, pressed
 (see page 10) and cut
 into cubes
400g/14oz can chickpeas,
 rinsed and drained
8 cherry tomatoes, halved
400g/14oz baby spinach
a handful of Thai basil or
 coriander (cilantro),
 chopped
2 tbsp chopped roasted
 peanuts
boiled or steamed rice and
 lime wedges, to serve

This curry is both gluten and dairy-free as well as vegan-friendly.
You can make it as hot or as mild as you like, depending on the type
and quantity of curry paste you use.

1 Heat the oil in a large saucepan set over a medium heat. Cook the onion,
 red pepper, garlic and ginger for 6–8 minutes, stirring occasionally, until
 the vegetables start to soften.

2 Stir in the curry paste and turmeric and cook for 1 minute. Add the
 coconut milk, stock and peanut butter and bring to the boil. Reduce
 the heat and simmer gently for 10 minutes.

3 Stir in the tofu, chickpeas and cherry tomatoes and cook gently for
 5 minutes, then add the spinach and cook for 2 minutes until it wilts
 and turns bright green. By this time the sauce should have reduced
 and thickened.

4 Serve the curry, sprinkled with the basil or coriander and chopped
 peanuts, on a bed of rice with some lime wedges for squeezing.

OR YOU CAN TRY THIS...

– Add some broccoli or cauliflower florets, aubergine (eggplant) or okra.
– Use shredded kale or spring greens instead of spinach.

SPICY TOFU STIR-FRY

SERVES: 4 | **PREP:** 10 MINUTES | **MARINATE:** 30 MINUTES | **COOK:** 10-12 MINUTES

500g/1lb 2oz extra-firm
   or firm tofu, pressed
   (see page 10) and cut
   into large cubes
2 garlic cloves, crushed
1 tsp Sichuan peppercorns,
   crushed
5 tbsp vegetable oil
400g/14oz thin rice noodles
1 large green (bell) pepper,
   deseeded and thinly sliced
300g/10oz chestnut
   mushrooms, quartered
1 bunch of spring onions
   (scallions), trimmed and
   halved lengthways
4 small or baby pak choi
   (bok choy), trimmed and
   halved lengthways
150g/5oz mangetout
   (snow peas) or sugar snap
   peas, trimmed
2 tbsp soy sauce or nam pla
   (Thai fish sauce)
sweet chilli sauce, for
   drizzling

You can buy hot Sichuan peppercorns in most supermarkets as well as delis and specialist Asian food stores.

1 Put the tofu, garlic, crushed peppercorns and oil into a bowl, and mix gently to coat the tofu. Leave to marinate for 30 minutes.

2 Cook the noodles following the pack instructions. Drain.

3 Drain the marinating liquid into a non-stick wok or deep frying pan (skillet) and set over a medium to high heat. When it's hot, add the green pepper and stir-fry for 2 minutes. Add the mushrooms and cook for 2–3 minutes until golden brown.

4 Stir in the spring onions, pak choi and mangetout or sugar snap peas and stir-fry for about 2 minutes, or until just tender. Stir in the rice noodles and soy sauce or nam pla and divide between 4 serving bowls.

5 Add the tofu to the hot wok and fry, turning gently once or twice, for 3–4 minutes, or until golden all over. Remove and spoon over the noodles and vegetables. Serve immediately, drizzled with sweet chilli sauce.

OR YOU CAN TRY THIS...
– Add some shredded or diced chilli.
– Omit the noodles and serve with boiled rice.
– Add some beansprouts, shredded carrots or red and yellow peppers.
– Stir in 1–2 tablespoons rice wine or vinegar.

STICKY STIR-FRIED TOFU & AUBERGINE

SERVES: 4-6 | **PREP:** 10 MINUTES | **COOK:** 25 MINUTES | **STAND:** 5-10 MINUTES

For the coconut rice:
vegetable oil, for brushing
450g/1lb (2 cups) Thai
　　fragrant jasmine rice
a pinch of salt
480ml/16fl oz (2 cups)
　　coconut milk

For the stir-fry:
2 tbsp sesame oil
400g/14oz marinated tofu,
　　cut into cubes
1 bunch of spring onions
　　(scallions), sliced
2 garlic cloves, crushed
1 red bird's eye chilli,
　　shredded
2.5cm/1in piece fresh root
　　ginger, peeled and diced
8 baby aubergines
　　(eggplants), quartered
90ml/3fl oz (generous ¼ cup)
　　vegetable stock (broth)
2 tbsp dark soy sauce
1 tbsp rice wine vinegar
2 tbsp mirin
2 tsp brown sugar or
　　palm sugar
2 tsp cornflour (cornstarch)
juice of ½ lime
a few sprigs of coriander
　　(cilantro), chopped
2 tbsp sesame seeds

This delicious stir-fry is elevated into something special by being served with fragrant coconut rice. If you're weight-conscious you can use reduced-fat coconut milk without any loss of flavour.

1 For the coconut rice, brush the bottom and sides of a heavy-based saucepan with oil and add the rice, salt, coconut milk and 420ml/14fl oz (1¾ cups) water. Stir and bring to the boil over a medium to high heat, then reduce the heat to a simmer and cook, covered with a lid, for 15 minutes, or until the rice has absorbed nearly all the liquid. Remove from the heat and leave, covered, for 5–10 minutes.

2 Meanwhile, heat the oil in a non-stick wok over a high heat and stir-fry the tofu for 4–5 minutes until golden. Remove and drain on kitchen paper (paper towels).

3 Add the spring onions, garlic, chilli and ginger and stir-fry for 2 minutes. Add the aubergines and cook for 2–3 minutes, then reduce the heat to low and add the stock. Cook gently for 10 minutes, or until the aubergines are tender.

4 Add the soy sauce, vinegar, mirin and sugar, turn up the heat to medium and cook for 2–3 minutes. Blend the cornflour with 2 tablespoons cold water and add to the pan. Stir gently for 1–2 minutes until the sauce thickens. Stir in the tofu and lime juice.

5 Fluff up the rice with a fork and divide between 4 serving bowls. Spoon the sticky tofu and aubergine mixture over the top and sprinkle with coriander and sesame seeds. Serve immediately.

OR YOU CAN TRY THIS...

– Use pressed extra-firm or firm tofu instead of marinated.
– Add some pak choi (bok choy) or baby spinach.
– If you can't get baby aubergines, cut a large aubergine into batons.

STIR-FRIED GINGER TOFU & GREENS

SERVES: 4 | **PREP:** 10 MINUTES | **COOK:** 15–20 MINUTES

75g/3oz (½ cup) cashews

3 tbsp groundnut (peanut) oil

450g/1lb marinated tofu, cut into cubes

4 garlic cloves, crushed

1 red chilli, shredded

5cm/2in piece fresh root ginger, peeled and diced

1 bunch of spring onions (scallions), sliced

400g/14oz spinach, kale or spring greens, shredded

200g/7oz Tenderstem® or purple-sprouting broccoli, trimmed

2 tbsp soy sauce, e.g. sweet kecap manis

1 tbsp hoisin sauce

1 tsp clear honey or agave syrup

dash of rice wine vinegar

boiled rice or rice noodles, to serve

This is a great and healthy way to warm up on a cold day in winter or early spring. You can use any green leafy vegetables for a big hit of vitamin C. The ginger has anti-viral properties and will help combat colds and infections.

1 Set a non-stick frying pan (skillet) over a medium heat and when it's hot add the cashews. Dry-fry, tossing them gently, for 1–2 minutes until golden brown and fragrant. Remove from the pan immediately, before they burn; set aside.

2 Heat the oil in a non-stick wok or large, deep frying pan set over a medium heat. When it's hot, start adding the tofu, in batches, and cook, turning occasionally, for 4–5 minutes, or until golden all over. Remove and drain on kitchen paper (paper towels).

3 Add the garlic, chilli and ginger and stir-fry for 1 minute without browning. Add the spring onions, greens and broccoli and stir-fry for 4 minutes, or until just tender but still a little crisp.

4 Stir in the soy sauce, hoisin sauce, honey or agave and vinegar. Add the tofu and cook for 1 minute.

5 Divide between 4 shallow serving bowls and scatter the toasted cashews over the top. Serve immediately with boiled rice or noodles.

OR YOU CAN TRY THIS...

– Add some quartered pak choi (bok choy).

– Add some sliced or quartered mushrooms.

– Use sesame oil instead of groundnut oil.

– Squeeze some lime wedges over the stir-fried tofu and greens.

SINGAPORE NOODLES WITH TOFU

SERVES: 4 | **PREP:** 15 MINUTES | **COOK:** 12-15 MINUTES

250g/9oz fine rice noodles
2 tbsp light soy sauce
1 tbsp rice wine or dry sherry
a pinch of sugar
3 tbsp groundnut (peanut)
    or sunflower oil
400g extra-firm or firm
    tofu, pressed (see page
    10) and cut into strips
1 bunch of spring onions
    (scallions), thickly sliced
2 garlic cloves, crushed
1 red chilli, deseeded and
    shredded
2.5cm/1in piece fresh root
    ginger, peeled and diced
1 red (bell) pepper, deseeded
    and thinly sliced
150g/5oz (1½ cups)
    beansprouts
100g/3½oz mangetout
    (snow peas), trimmed
1 tbsp Madras curry paste
a handful of coriander
    (cilantro), chopped
2 tbsp chopped roasted
    peanuts
sweet chilli sauce, for
    drizzling
lime wedges, to serve

The secret to successful stir-fries is to prepare everything in advance and line up the ingredients within easy reach of the hob. Don't use flat rice noodles for this dish – you really do need the thin rice vermicelli.

1 Cook the rice noodles following the pack instructions. Drain and toss in the soy sauce, rice wine or sherry and sugar.

2 Meanwhile, heat 2 tablespoons of the oil in a non-stick wok or large frying pan (skillet) set over a medium to high heat. Add the tofu and cook, stirring often, for about 5 minutes until golden all over. Remove and drain on kitchen paper (paper towels).

3 Add the remaining oil to the wok and stir-fry the spring onions, garlic, chilli, ginger and red pepper for 2 minutes. Add the beansprouts and mangetout and stir-fry for 2 minutes.

4 Stir in the curry paste and cook for 1 minute, then add the noodles together with 5–6 tablespoons water. Toss everything together and cook for 2 minutes or so until the liquid reduces. Gently stir in the tofu.

5 Divide between 4 shallow serving bowls and sprinkle with coriander and peanuts. Drizzle with chilli sauce and serve immediately with lime wedges.

OR YOU CAN TRY THIS...
– Use curry powder instead of curry paste.
– Add some sliced mushrooms, thin green beans, peas or water chestnuts.

TOFU BURRITOS

SERVES: 4 | **PREP:** 15 MINUTES | **COOK:** 30-35 MINUTES

2 tbsp olive oil
1 large red onion, chopped
3 garlic cloves, crushed
1 red (bell) pepper,
    deseeded and diced
1 yellow (bell) pepper,
    deseeded and diced
1 jalapeño chilli, diced
1 tsp smoked paprika
½ tsp ground cumin
350g/12oz ripe tomatoes,
    chopped
400g/14oz can black beans,
    rinsed and drained
4 large soft tortillas
1 small bunch of spring
    onions (scallions),
    chopped
200g/7oz extra-firm or firm
    tofu, pressed (see page 10)
50g/2oz (½ cup) grated
    Cheddar or Monterey
    Jack cheese
few sprigs of coriander
    (cilantro), chopped
salt and freshly ground
    black pepper
lime wedges, natural
    yoghurt and guacamole,
    to serve

This Tex-Mex favourite is given a new twist by adding crumbled tofu. Vegans can use grated vegan cheese-style block and serve the burritos with non-dairy soya or coconut yoghurt.

1 Preheat the oven to 180°C, 350°F, gas mark 4.

2 For the filling, heat the olive oil in a non-stick frying pan (skillet) over a low heat. Add the onion, garlic, peppers and chilli and cook gently, stirring occasionally, for 6–8 minutes until softened.

3 Add the spices, tomatoes and beans and simmer for 10 minutes, or until the sauce reduces and thickens. Season to taste with salt and pepper.

4 Spoon a little filling down the centre of each tortilla – don't use it all. Sprinkle with the spring onions and then, using your fingers, crumble the tofu over the top. Fold each tortilla around the filling like a parcel, folding in the sides to seal it. Arrange the burritos, seam-side down, in an ovenproof dish.

5 Pour the remaining filling over the top and sprinkle with the grated cheese. Bake in the oven for 15 minutes until golden brown and bubbling.

6 Serve the burritos, sprinkled with coriander, with lime wedges for squeezing and some yoghurt and guacamole on the side.

OR YOU CAN TRY THIS...

– Serve with salsa or pico de gallo.
– Instead of guacamole, just mash a ripe avocado with some lime juice.
– Use refried beans, kidney beans or chickpeas instead of black beans.

JAPANESE TOFU STIR-FRY

SERVES: 4 | **PREP:** 10 MINUTES | **COOK:** 10-12 MINUTES

2 tbsp sesame seeds

400g/14oz soba or
    wholewheat noodles

2 tbsp sesame oil

350g/12oz extra-firm
    or firm tofu, pressed
    (see page 10) and cut
    into strips

a good pinch of dried chilli
    flakes

300g/10oz (2 cups) frozen
    edamame (soy) beans

2 pak choi (bok choy),
    trimmed and sliced

2 tbsp Japanese soy sauce

2 tbsp rice wine vinegar

3 garlic cloves, crushed

2 tbsp grated fresh root
    ginger

juice of 1 lime

1 tsp caster (superfine) sugar

4 spring onions (scallions),
    shredded

The toasted sesame seeds add crunch as well as their distinctive flavour to this quick stir-fry. If wished, use a packet of smoked or marinated tofu.

1 Heat a small non-stick frying pan (skillet) over a medium to high heat. Add the sesame seeds to the pan and dry-fry for 1–2 minutes, tossing gently, until fragrant and golden. Remove immediately, before they burn.

2 Cook the noodles following the pack instructions.

3 Heat the oil in a non-stick wok or deep frying pan and cook the tofu, turning occasionally, for about 5 minutes until golden all over. Remove and drain on kitchen paper (paper towels). Sprinkle with the sesame seeds and chilli flakes.

4 Add the edamame beans and pak choi to the hot wok and stir-fry for 2 minutes. Stir in the noodles, soy sauce, vinegar, garlic, ginger, lime juice and sugar and heat through gently for 1 minute.

5 Divide between 4 shallow bowls and serve topped with the tofu and sprinkled with shredded spring onions.

OR YOU CAN TRY THIS...

– Use rice, buckwheat or egg noodles.
– Vary the vegetables: try broccoli, green peas, kale, spinach or spring greens.
– Add some heat with a diced chilli.
– Flavour with miso paste or some tamari sauce.

CRUNCHY TOFU & PEANUT STIR-FRY

SERVES: 4 | **PREP:** 15 MINUTES | **COOK:** 10 MINUTES

For the peanut butter sauce:
2 tbsp smooth peanut butter
2 tbsp soft brown sugar
3 garlic cloves, crushed
1 tbsp grated fresh root
   ginger
1 red bird's eye chilli, diced
2 tbsp tamari
1 tbsp groundnut (peanut)
   oil
juice of ½ lime

For the stir-fry:
400g/14oz extra-firm tofu,
   pressed (see page 10)
   and cut into cubes
2 tbsp cornflour (cornstarch)
1 tsp Sichuan peppercorns,
   crushed
coarse sea salt
2 tbsp vegetable oil
150g/5oz baby sweetcorn
150g/5oz mangetout
   (snow peas), halved and
   trimmed
1 bunch of spring onions
   (scallions), sliced
   diagonally
4 tbsp roasted peanuts
   (whole or crushed)
boiled rice or noodles,
   to serve
lime wedges, to serve

This stir-fry of crispy tofu and crunchy peanuts and vegetables makes an easy weekday supper. It's quite hot but you could leave out the chilli in the peanut butter sauce if you'd like a milder spiced dish.

1 Combine all the ingredients for the peanut butter sauce in a blender and blitz until smooth.

2 Put the tofu cubes in a bowl with the cornflour, crushed peppercorns and a pinch of salt. Turn gently to coat it all over.

3 Heat the oil in a non-stick wok or frying pan (skillet) set over a medium to high heat. Add the tofu and fry for 4–5 minutes, turning occasionally until golden brown all over. Remove and drain on kitchen paper (paper towels).

4 Add the sweetcorn, mangetout and spring onions to the wok and stir-fry for 2–3 minutes. Stir in the peanut butter sauce and cook gently for 1–2 minutes until heated through. Stir in the tofu.

5 Serve the stir-fry on a bed of rice or noodles, sprinkled with peanuts and with lime wedges for squeezing.

OR YOU CAN TRY THIS...
– Add some shredded greens, such as pak choi (bok choy), kale or spinach.
– Use cashew butter and cashew nuts.
– Substitute soy sauce for the tamari.
– Serve sprinkled with chopped Thai basil or coriander (cilantro).

TOFU, BROCCOLI & AVOCADO RICE BOWL

SERVES: 4 | **PREP:** 10 MINUTES | **COOK:** 20-30 MINUTES

225g/8oz (1 cup) brown rice
400g/14oz smoked tofu
1 tsp smoked paprika
3 tbsp olive oil
1 red onion, chopped
2 garlic cloves crushed
400g/14oz can kidney
    beans, rinsed and drained
250g/9oz baby plum
    tomatoes
a good glug of balsamic
    vinegar, plus extra for
    drizzling
250g/9oz Tenderstem®
    broccoli or calabrese
1 large ripe avocado, peeled,
    stoned (pitted) and sliced
a handful of coriander
    (cilantro) or basil, chopped
salt and freshly ground
    black pepper

These colourful bowls make a delicious and healthy supper. The crispy tofu, creamy avocado, fresh-tasting broccoli and piquant beans and tomatoes are a great combo with the nutty brown rice.

1 Preheat the oven to 220°C, 425°F, gas mark 7.

2 Cook the brown rice following the pack instructions.

3 Blot the tofu with kitchen paper (paper towels) and cut into fingers. Stir the paprika into 1 tablespoon of the olive oil and brush over the tofu. Season with salt and pepper. Arrange the tofu in a single layer on a baking tray (cookie sheet) and bake in the preheated oven for 15 minutes, or until golden and crisp.

4 Meanwhile, heat the remaining oil in a non-stick frying pan (skillet) over a medium heat and cook the onion and garlic, stirring occasionally, for 6–8 minutes until tender. Stir in the beans and tomatoes and cook for 4–5 minutes until the beans are hot and the tomatoes have softened. Season with salt and pepper and add a little balsamic vinegar, to taste.

5 If using Tenderstem® broccoli, trim the stems and cut them in half lengthways; for calabrese, cut into small florets. Blanch the broccoli in a saucepan of boiling water for 2 minutes and drain well, or steam until just tender but slightly crisp.

6 Divide the brown rice between 4 bowls and add the bean and tomato mixture, baked tofu, broccoli and avocado. Drizzle with balsamic vinegar and sprinkle with coriander or basil. Serve immediately.

OR YOU CAN TRY THIS...
– Add some diced chilli to the beans and tomatoes.
– Drizzle with soy sauce or pomegranate molasses instead of balsamic.
– Instead of broccoli, use fine green beans or sugar snap peas.
– Use quinoa or mixed grains instead of rice.

TOFU TEMPURA

SERVES: 4 | **PREP:** 15 MINUTES | **COOK:** 12-15 MINUTES

For the dipping sauce:
3 tbsp light soy sauce
1 tbsp rice wine vinegar
1 tbsp water
1 tsp sesame oil
juice of ½ lime
1 tsp caster (superfine) sugar
2 tsp grated fresh root
    ginger

For the batter:
225g/8oz plain (all-purpose)
    flour
30g/1oz (¼ cup) cornflour
    (cornstarch)
4 tsp bicarbonate of soda
    (baking soda)
½ tsp salt
600ml/1 pint (2½ cups)
    ice-cold sparkling mineral
    water

For the tempura:
vegetable oil, for deep-frying
400g/14oz extra-firm or
    firm tofu, pressed
    (see page 10) and cut
    into cubes
freshly ground black pepper
1 red bird's eye chilli,
    deseeded and finely
    shredded
boiled rice and stir-fried
    vegetables, to serve

This is really easy to make, especially if you have a deep fat fryer. Unlike most other batters, this one has to be very light and crisp so it barely clings to the tofu. Serve the tempura with stir-fried greens, such as pak choi (bok choy) and mangetout (snow peas), sprinkled with sesame seeds.

1 Combine all the ingredients for the dipping sauce in a small bowl and whisk together.

2 For the batter, sift the flour, cornflour, bicarbonate of soda and salt into a large mixing bowl. Whisk in the chilled sparkling water but be careful not to over-whisk as you need a few lumps.

3 Preheat the oven to 120°C, 250°F, gas mark ½. Heat the oil in a deep, heavy-based saucepan or deep fat fryer until it reaches 180°C/350°F. Either use a sugar thermometer to check the temperature or add a 1cm/½in cube of bread – the oil is ready when the bread cube sizzles and turns brown in 25 seconds.

4 Season the tofu with black pepper. Quickly dip some of the cubes into the batter, shaking off any excess. Deep-fry in batches, a few cubes at a time, for 4–5 minutes until crisp and light golden. Remove with a slotted spoon, drain on kitchen paper (paper towels) and keep warm in the oven while you fry the rest.

5 Divide the hot tofu between 4 serving plates and sprinkle with the shredded chilli. Serve immediately with the dipping sauce and some boiled rice and stir-fried vegetables.

ROASTED VEGETABLE & TOFU TRAYBAKE

SERVES: 4 | **PREP:** 15 MINUTES | **MARINATE:** 30 MINUTES | **COOK:** 40 MINUTES

400g/14oz extra-firm
   or firm tofu, pressed
   (see page 10)
2 tbsp light soy sauce
1 tbsp clear honey
1 tsp sesame oil
2 garlic cloves, crushed
1 tbsp grated fresh root
   ginger
a pinch of crushed chilli
   flakes
450g/1lb sweet potatoes,
   peeled and cut into chunks
2 red onions, cut into wedges
2 red or yellow (bell)
   peppers, deseeded and
   cut into chunks
300g/10oz baby carrots,
   trimmed and scrubbed
olive oil for, drizzling
salt and freshly ground
   black pepper
toasted sesame seeds, for
   sprinkling
sweet chilli sauce or soy
   sauce, for drizzling
   (optional)

TIP: Vegans can use agave syrup, maple syrup or brown sugar instead of honey.

Everyone loves a traybake. They are so versatile and easy to prepare and cook and washing up is kept to a minimum. This is great for weekday evenings when you get home from work and don't want to spend a lot of time in the kitchen.

1 Preheat the oven to 200°C, 400°F, gas mark 6.

2 Cut the tofu into slices and place in a shallow bowl. Combine the soy sauce, honey, sesame oil, garlic, ginger and chilli flakes in a small jug, whisk and pour over the tofu. Leave to marinate for 30 minutes.

3 Arrange all the vegetables, in a single layer, in a large roasting pan and drizzle with olive oil. Season lightly with salt and pepper. Roast in the oven for 25 minutes.

4 Add the tofu to the vegetables in the pan and pour any remaining marinade over the top. Return to the oven for 15 minutes, or until the tofu is golden brown and the vegetables are tender.

5 Divide between 4 serving plates, sprinkle with toasted sesame seeds and serve immediately. If wished, drizzle with sweet chilli sauce or soy sauce.

OR YOU CAN TRY THIS...

– Try other vegetables: pumpkin, swede (rutabaga), butternut squash, parsnips, aubergine (eggplant), tomatoes, green beans or asparagus.
– Drizzle with balsamic vinegar or pomegranate molasses.
– Sprinkle with chopped coriander (cilantro).

SPICY DEVILLED TOFU & VEGETABLE KEBABS

SERVES: 4 | **PREP:** 15 MINUTES | **MARINATE:** 15 MINUTES | **COOK:** 8-10 MINUTES

For the spicy devilled marinade:

2 tbsp tomato purée (paste)
2 tbsp Worcestershire sauce
1 tbsp olive oil
juice of ½ lemon
1 tbsp soft brown sugar
1 tbsp Dijon mustard
2 garlic cloves, crushed
1 tsp paprika
1 tsp cayenne pepper

For the kebabs:

400g/14oz extra-firm tofu, pressed (see page 10)
2 red onions, cut into wedges
2 red or yellow (bell) peppers, deseeded and cut into chunks
2 courgettes (zucchini), cut into chunks
olive oil, for brushing
salt and freshly ground black pepper
a few sprigs of flat-leaf parsley, chopped
boiled rice and salad, to serve

You can make these kebabs as hot and spicy as you wish. Turn up the heat by adding some Sriracha or other hot sauce, chilli powder or extra cayenne pepper.

1 Combine all the ingredients for the spicy devilled marinade in a large bowl and mix together. Cut the tofu into cubes and add to the mixture. Stir gently until it's coated all over with the marinade. Cover and leave to marinate for at least 15 minutes.

2 Meanwhile, soak 8 bamboo or wooden skewers in cold water to prevent them from burning during cooking.

3 Thread the marinated tofu and prepared vegetables alternately onto the soaked skewers. Brush the vegetables with olive oil and season lightly with salt and pepper.

4 Preheat a barbecue or a grill (broiler) to high. Place the kebabs over hot coals on the barbecue or put them in a foil-lined grill pan and place under the preheated grill. Cook for 8–10 minutes, turning them occasionally and basting with any leftover marinade, or until the vegetables are tender and the tofu is brown and sticky.

5 Sprinkle the parsley over the kebabs and serve with rice and salad.

OR YOU CAN TRY THIS...

– Use other vegetables: cherry tomatoes, mushrooms, baby corn, aubergine (eggplant) and squash.
– Drizzle with balsamic vinegar or sprinkle with lemon juice.

SMOKED TOFU & LENTILS WITH ROASTED PEPPERS

SERVES: 4 | **PREP:** 10 MINUTES | **COOK:** 30 MINUTES

2 large red or yellow (bell) peppers, deseeded and cut into large chunks

3 tbsp olive oil, plus extra for drizzling

400g/14oz smoked tofu, sliced

1 tsp smoked paprika

200g/7oz (generous 1 cup) Puy or green lentils

1 large onion, chopped

2 large carrots, finely diced

2 celery sticks, diced

2 garlic cloves, crushed

300g/10oz baby plum tomatoes, halved

juice of 1 lemon

2 tbsp balsamic vinegar

a handful of flat-leaf parsley, chopped

200g/7oz fine green beans, trimmed

3 tbsp green pesto, for drizzling

salt and freshly ground black pepper

Lentils have a wonderful earthy flavour and are surprisingly filling. Don't use the small red ones in this recipe as they cook to a purée and don't retain their shape – you need Puy or green ones.

1 Preheat the oven to 200°C, 400°F, gas mark 6.

2 Place the red peppers on a large baking tray (cookie sheet) and drizzle with olive oil. Add the tofu, dusting it with the smoked paprika. Lightly season with salt and pepper. Bake in the preheated oven for about 30 minutes, or until the peppers are tender and slightly charred and the tofu is golden.

3 Meanwhile, put the lentils into a saucepan and cover them with cold water. Bring to the boil, reduce the heat and simmer gently for 20 minutes, or until they are tender but still have a little bite. Drain and refresh under running cold water.

4 While the lentils are cooking, heat 2 tablespoons of the olive oil in a large non-stick frying pan (skillet) over a low heat. Add the onion, carrots, celery and garlic and cook for 8–10 minutes, stirring occasionally, until softened.

5 Add the tomatoes and cooked lentils to the frying pan and cook for 5 minutes, stirring occasionally. If the lentils start to stick, add a little water. Stir in the lemon juice, balsamic vinegar and parsley. Season to taste with salt and pepper.

6 Cook the green beans in a saucepan of boiling water for 3–4 minutes until just tender but not too soft. Drain, refresh under running cold water and add to the lentils.

7 Stir the remaining olive oil into the lentil mixture and divide between 4 serving plates. Top with the roasted red peppers and tofu. Drizzle with pesto and eat immediately.

CRISPY TOFU & QUINOA BOWL

SERVES: 4 | **PREP:** 15 MINUTES | **COOK:** 25 MINUTES

75g/3oz (½ cup) cashews
480ml/16fl oz (2 cups)
    vegetable stock (broth)
200g/7oz (generous 1 cup)
    quinoa
300g/10oz broccoli, cut
    into florets
200g/7oz mangetout
    (snow peas), trimmed
1 tbsp groundnut
    (peanut) oil
1 bunch of spring onions
    (scallions), sliced
1 large red (bell) pepper,
    deseeded and diced
2 garlic cloves, crushed
2.5cm/1in piece fresh root
    ginger, peeled and diced
1 red bird's eye chilli,
    shredded
3 tbsp light soy sauce
grated zest and juice of
    1 lime
continued >

You can eat this dish hot from the wok or leave it to cool and take some to work with you in a sealed container for a nutritious packed lunch.

1 Place a small non-stick frying pan (skillet) over a medium heat. Add the cashews to the hot pan, gently tossing and turning them, for 1–2 minutes until fragrant and golden brown. Remove from the pan immediately, before they burn.

2 Heat the stock and when it starts to boil, add the quinoa. Cover and simmer gently for 15 minutes until tender, most of the liquid has been absorbed and the 'sprouts' pop out of the quinoa seeds. Remove from the heat and set aside for 5 minutes before draining off any liquid. Fluff up the quinoa with a fork.

3 Meanwhile, blanch the broccoli and mangetout in a saucepan of boiling water for 1 minute. Plunge into a bowl of iced water, then drain and set aside.

4 Heat the oil in a non-stick wok or large frying pan over a medium heat and stir-fry the spring onions, red pepper, garlic, ginger and chilli for 2 minutes. Add the soy sauce, lime juice, broccoli, mangetout and tomatoes. Stir-fry for 1–2 minutes, then stir in the quinoa. Season to taste with salt and pepper.

200g/7oz baby plum
   tomatoes, quartered
400g/14oz extra-firm
   or firm tofu, pressed
   (see page 10) and cut
   into cubes
3 tbsp cornflour (cornstarch)
1 tbsp vegetable oil
a handful of coriander
   (cilantro), chopped
salt and freshly ground
   black pepper

5 Season the tofu with salt and pepper and coat with the cornflour. Heat the oil in a large non-stick frying pan over a medium to high heat and fry the tofu, turning when it's golden underneath, for 4–5 minutes, or until crispy. Remove and drain on kitchen paper (paper towels).

6 Divide the stir-fried quinoa between 4 shallow bowls and spoon the tofu over the top. Sprinkle with the toasted cashews and coriander and serve.

OR YOU CAN TRY THIS...

– Drizzle some sweet chilli sauce over the top.
– You can deep-fry, bake or griddle the tofu.
– Use brown rice instead of quinoa.

HOISIN TOFU FINGERS & EGG-FRIED RICE

SERVES: 4 | **PREP:** 10 MINUTES | **COOK:** 10-12 MINUTES

For the tofu fingers:
vegetable oil, for brushing
400g/14oz extra-firm or
    firm tofu, pressed
    (see page 10)
3 tbsp hoisin sauce
1 tbsp sesame seeds

For the egg-fried rice:
2 tbsp vegetable oil, e.g.
    sunflower or groundnut
    (peanut)
1cm/½in piece fresh root
    ginger, peeled and diced
2 garlic cloves, crushed
1 bunch of spring onions
    (scallions), sliced
    diagonally
100g/3½oz (⅔ cup) frozen
    peas, defrosted
400g/14oz (generous
    1½ cups) cooked white
    or brown rice
2 medium free-range eggs,
    beaten
2 tbsp light soy sauce

TIP: To quickly defrost
the peas, rinse them in a
colander under running
warm water.

This is a delicious way to use up leftover cooked rice. It also uses store-cupboard ingredients and staples from the fridge and freezer for a really simple, delicious meal.

1 Preheat the grill (broiler) to high. Line a grill pan with foil and brush lightly with oil.

2 Cut the tofu into fingers and brush both sides with the hoisin sauce. Place them in the lined pan and sprinkle with half the sesame seeds. Cook under the grill for 5–6 minutes until browned. Turn the tofu fingers over and sprinkle with the remaining sesame seeds. Cook under the grill for a few more minutes until crisp and browned.

3 For the egg-fried rice, heat the oil in a non-stick wok or deep frying pan over a medium to high heat and stir-fry the ginger, garlic and spring onions for 2 minutes without browning. Add the peas and cook for 1 minute, then stir in the rice and keep stirring and tossing for 1–2 minutes until heated through and coated in oil.

4 Pour the beaten eggs into the middle of the wok and keep stirring until they start to set and scramble in to the rice. Add the soy sauce.

5 Divide the egg-fried rice between 4 serving bowls and serve topped with the hoisin tofu fingers.

OR YOU CAN TRY THIS...
– Add some sesame oil or diced chilli to the egg-fried rice.
– Stir some blanched vegetables into the rice, e.g. broccoli florets, diced green beans or sliced sautéed mushrooms.

MAPO TOFU & SHIITAKE MUSHROOMS

SERVES: 4 | **PREP:** 15 MINUTES | **COOK:** 15-20 MINUTES

2 tbsp Sichuan peppercorns
500g/1lb 2oz extra-firm or
   firm silken tofu
2 tbsp vegetable oil
1 red bird's eye chilli,
   shredded
2.5cm/1in piece fresh root
   ginger, peeled and diced
2 garlic cloves, crushed
1 bunch of spring onions
   (scallions), thinly sliced
450g/1lb shiitake
   mushrooms, diced
1 tbsp douchi
50g/2oz doubanjiang
1 tbsp sugar
400ml/14fl oz (scant 1¾ cups)
   vegetable stock (broth)
1 tbsp cornflour (cornstarch)
1–2 tbsp soy sauce
2 tbsp toasted sesame seeds
a few sprigs of coriander
   (cilantro), chopped
boiled rice, to serve

**This classic Sichuan dish is seriously hot. To be really authentic
you will need some *douchi* (fermented black beans) and *doubanjiang*
(a fermented broad bean paste). Both are available in specialist Asian
stores or online.**

1 Place a small non-stick frying pan (skillet) over a medium to high
   heat. Add the peppercorns and toss gently for about 2 minutes
   until they release their aroma. Remove from the pan and grind to
   a powder in a pestle and mortar or spice grinder.

2 Cut the tofu into cubes. Gently add them to a large saucepan of
   boiling salted water and boil for 1 minute. Remove with a slotted
   spoon and drain. Set aside.

3 Heat the oil in a non-stick wok or large frying pan over a medium
   heat and stir-fry the chilli, ginger, garlic and spring onions for
   1 minute. Add the mushrooms and stir-fry for about 3 minutes
   until golden brown.

4 Stir in the douchi, doubanjiang, sugar and ground peppercorns.
   Cook for 2 minutes, add the stock and bring to the boil. Reduce
   the heat and blend the cornflour with a little cold water to a smooth
   paste. Add to the wok, stirring until the mixture thickens. Add some
   soy sauce, to taste, and gently stir in the tofu. Cook gently for
   4–5 minutes.

5 Serve over boiled rice, sprinkled with sesame seeds and coriander.

TIP: If the sauce is too
liquid for your taste, just
blend another spoonful of
cornflour with some water
and stir into the wok.

TOFU TIKKA MASALA

SERVES: 4 | **PREP:** 15 MINUTES | **MARINATE:** 30 MINUTES | **COOK:** 40 MINUTES

For the marinated tofu:
1 tsp ground turmeric
1 tsp ground coriander
½ tsp ground cumin
1 tsp garam masala
½ tsp chilli powder
a handful of coriander
   (cilantro), chopped
4 tbsp thick Greek yoghurt
400g/14oz extra-firm or firm
   tofu, pressed (see page 10)
   and cut into cubes

For the curry:
3 tbsp vegetable oil
1 cinnamon stick
1 tsp cumin seeds
1 large onion, finely chopped
3 garlic cloves, crushed
2.5cm/1in piece fresh root
   ginger, peeled and chopped
1 tsp curry powder
400g/14oz can plum tomatoes
a pinch of sugar
360ml/12fl oz (1½ cups)
   vegetable stock (broth)
4 tbsp double (heavy) cream
   or crème fraîche
1 tsp paprika
4 tbsp chopped coriander
   (cilantro)
boiled rice or naan bread,
   to serve

Don't be put off by the long list of ingredients – many of them are just the spices you keep in your store cupboard. This is so easy to make and cook and well worth the effort. Vegans can substitute dairy-free yoghurt alternative for the cream or crème fraîche.

1 For the marinated tofu, mix the ground spices and coriander with the yoghurt in a large bowl. Add the tofu cubes, stirring gently until well coated. Cover and chill in the fridge for at least 30 minutes.

2 Heat 2 tablespoons of the oil in a large non-stick frying pan (skillet) set over a medium heat and add the cinnamon stick and cumin seeds. Cook for 1–2 minutes and then add the onion, garlic and ginger. Cook for about 10 minutes, stirring occasionally, until the onion is tender and golden. Stir in the curry powder and cook for 1 minute.

3 Add the tomatoes, sugar and stock and reduce the heat to a simmer. Cover and cook gently for 15 minutes, or until the sauce reduces and thickens. Discard the cinnamon stick. If wished, you can purée the sauce with a hand-held electric blender until smooth. Stir in the cream or crème fraîche and paprika.

4 Take the tofu out of the fridge and heat the remaining oil in a large non-stick frying pan over a medium heat. Add the tofu and the marinade and cook for 3–4 minutes until brown underneath. Turn the cubes over and cook, stirring occasionally, until browned all over.

5 Gently stir the tofu into the curry and divide between 4 serving plates. Sprinkle with coriander and serve with rice or naan bread.

CURRIED TOFU & PUMPKIN RICE BOWLS

SERVES: 4 | **PREP:** 15 MINUTES | **COOK:** 30-35 MINUTES

3 tbsp sunflower oil

400g/14oz extra-firm
 or firm tofu, pressed
 (see page 10) and cut
 into cubes

1 large red onion, finely
 chopped

3 garlic cloves, crushed

2.5cm/1in piece fresh root
 ginger, peeled and diced

1 red bird's eye chilli, diced

1 lemongrass stalk, bashed

450g/1lb pumpkin, peeled,
 deseeded and cut
 into 2cm/¾in cubes
 (prepared weight)

1 tsp ground turmeric

½ tsp garam masala

1 tsp cumin seeds

400ml/14fl oz can coconut
 milk

1 ripe mango, peeled, stoned
 (pitted) and cubed

300g/10oz baby spinach

juice of 1 lime

a handful of coriander
 (cilantro), chopped

salt and freshly ground black
 pepper

boiled basmati or brown
 rice, to serve

This mildly spiced curry has a velvety, creamy texture thanks to the coconut milk. For a healthier option substitute reduced-fat for full-fat coconut milk. It will taste just as good.

1 Heat 1 tablespoon of the oil in a large non-stick frying pan (skillet) over a medium to high heat. Cook the tofu, in batches, for 4–6 minutes, turning occasionally, until golden all over. Remove from the pan and drain on kitchen paper (paper towels). Set aside.

2 Heat the remaining oil in a large saucepan over a low heat and cook the onion, garlic, ginger, chilli and lemongrass, stirring occasionally, for 6–8 minutes, or until the onion is tender and golden. Add the pumpkin and cook for 4–5 minutes, then stir in the ground spices and cumin seeds. Cook for 1 minute.

3 Pour in the coconut milk and bring to the boil. Reduce the heat to a simmer and cook gently for 10 minutes, or until the curry reduces and starts to thicken.

4 Stir in the mango, cooked tofu and spinach and cook for 2–3 minutes until the tofu is heated through and the spinach wilts. Stir in the lime juice and coriander, remove the lemongrass and season to taste with salt and pepper.

5 Divide between 4 shallow serving bowls and serve immediately with boiled rice.

OR YOU CAN TRY THIS...

– Use papaya (pawpaw) instead of mango.
– Instead of spices, just use some curry paste.
– If pumpkin is out of season, use sweet potato or squash.
– Serve with cucumber raita (see page 38) or some dairy-free coconut milk yoghurt alternative.

VEGAN TOFU & SPINACH LASAGNE

SERVES: 4-6 | **PREP:** 20 MINUTES | **COOK:** 50-60 MINUTES

For the roasted vegetables and tofu:

2 red onions, each cut into 6 wedges

1 aubergine (eggplant), cubed

2 courgettes (zucchini), thickly sliced

400g/14oz tomatoes, quartered

400g/14oz extra-firm or firm tofu, pressed (see page 10) and cut into cubes

olive oil, for drizzling

salt and freshly ground black pepper

For the white sauce:

4 tbsp cornflour (cornstarch)

600ml/1 pint (2½ cups) dairy-free milk alternative, e.g. soya or almond

a pinch of grated nutmeg

This lasagne is made with colourful roasted vegetables instead of a tomato sauce – the vegetables soften and add texture as well as flavour. You can use any grated hard vegan cheese-style block for this recipe – most supermarkets and health food stores now offer a choice.

1 Preheat the oven to 190°C, 375°F, gas mark 5.

2 Place the onions, aubergine, courgettes, tomatoes and tofu on a large baking tray (cookie sheet) and drizzle with olive oil. Season lightly with salt and pepper, then roast in the preheated oven for 25–30 minutes, until the vegetables are tender and the tofu is golden.

3 For the sauce, blend the cornflour and a little of the milk to a smooth paste in a small bowl or cup. Heat the remaining milk in a saucepan and as soon as it starts to boil, reduce the heat and stir in the cornflour mixture. Cook gently, stirring constantly with a wooden spoon, for 2–3 minutes until the sauce is thick and smooth and coats the back of the spoon. Remove from the heat and stir in the nutmeg. Season to taste with salt and pepper.

4 Cook the spinach with 1 tablespoon water in a large saucepan with a lid, shaking occasionally, for about 2 minutes until it wilts and turns green. Drain in a colander, pressing down with the back of a spoon to remove all the moisture. Chop coarsely and mix with the garlic and a ladleful of the white sauce.

For the lasagne:
1kg/2¼lb spinach, trimmed
2 garlic cloves, crushed
vegetable oil, for brushing
10–12 fresh vegan lasagne
    sheets
50g/2oz (½ cup) vegan hard
    cheese-style block, grated

5 Brush an ovenproof dish, approximately 20 x 30cm/8 x 12in, with vegetable oil. To assemble, layer the lasagne sheets, roasted vegetables and tofu, spinach and white sauce in the dish, finishing with a layer of lasagne and the remaining white sauce. Sprinkle with the grated cheese.

6 Bake in the oven for 25–30 minutes, or until crisp and golden brown. Cut into portions to serve.

OR YOU CAN TRY THIS...
– Use dried lasagne sheets instead of fresh.
– Vary the roasted vegetables: try pumpkin, sweet potato, red and yellow (bell) peppers, mushrooms or squash.

STIR-FRIED SESAME TOFU & NOODLES

SERVES: 4 | **PREP:** 15 MINUTES | **COOK:** 8–12 MINUTES

300g/10oz thin rice noodles
300g/10oz extra-firm
    or firm tofu, pressed
    (see page 10) and cut
    into cubes
1 medium free-range
    egg, beaten
3 tbsp cornflour (cornstarch)
5 tbsp black or white sesame
    seeds
2 tbsp vegetable oil, e.g.
    sunflower or rapeseed
1 head broccoli, cut into
    florets
1 red chilli, thinly sliced
juice of 1 lime
2 tbsp soy sauce
4 spring onions (scallions),
    shredded
salt and freshly ground
    black pepper

Another quick and easy stir-fry, perfect for when you don't have much time to cook. The sesame seeds give the tofu a delicious crunch when you bite into it.

1 Cook the noodles following the pack instructions.

2 Dip the tofu into the beaten egg, season with salt and pepper, then coat with the cornflour and sesame seeds. Set aside.

3 Heat half of the oil in a non-stick wok or large frying pan (skillet) over a medium to high heat and stir-fry the broccoli and chilli for 2–3 minutes until just tender but still crisp. Remove and keep warm.

4 Add the remaining oil to the wok and then cook the sesame coated tofu, a few pieces at a time, for 3–4 minutes until golden. Remove and drain on kitchen paper (paper towels).

5 Toss the noodles with the broccoli, lime juice and soy sauce. Divide between 4 shallow serving bowls and top with the sesame tofu and shredded spring onions. Serve immediately.

OR YOU CAN TRY THIS...

– Use egg noodles.
– Instead of broccoli, use shredded spring greens, kale or pak choi (bok choy).
– Add some shredded fresh root ginger and substitute a small lemon for the lime.
– To sweeten the dish, add a pinch of sugar or some sweet chilli sauce.

BAKING & DESSERTS

TOFU CHOCOLATE SMOOTHIE BOWL

SERVES: 2 | **PREP:** 10 MINUTES

225g/8oz silken tofu
120ml/4fl oz (½ cup)
    coconut or almond
    milk alternative
2 large frozen bananas
3 tbsp cocoa powder
1 tsp vanilla extract
coconut flakes, pomegranate
    seeds, sliced strawberries
    or sliced kiwi fruit,
    to decorate

You can eat this delicious smoothie bowl for a dessert, snack or breakfast – just remember to pop the bananas in the freezer in advance. It's packed with nourishing protein, vitamins and minerals. If it's not sweet enough for your liking, add a little stevia or maple or agave syrup, to taste.

1 Blend the tofu, coconut or almond milk alternative, bananas, cocoa powder and vanilla extract in a blender until thick, smooth and creamy. If it's too thick for your liking, add a little more milk.

2 Pour into 2 bowls and decorate with coconut flakes, pomegranate seeds, sliced strawberries or sliced kiwi fruit.

OR YOU CAN TRY THIS...

– Add some chocolate protein powder or some hemp seeds.
– Blend some frozen berries, e.g. blueberries, with the tofu, milk and bananas.
– Add 1–2 tablespoons peanut butter.
– Scatter with some crunchy granola.
– Decorate the top with rows of berries, passion fruit seeds, flaked almonds, chopped nuts, chia, sunflower and hemp seeds – whatever takes your fancy.

STRAWBERRY TOFU MOUSSE

SERVES: 4 | **PREP:** 10 MINUTES | **CHILL:** 3-4 HOURS

400g/14oz (2 cups)
   strawberries, sliced, plus
   extra whole strawberries,
   to decorate
225g/8oz firm tofu, roughly
   cubed
2 tbsp maple syrup
60g/2oz dark (bittersweet)
   chocolate, minimum
   70% cocoa solids, shaved

Firm tofu is used in this quick and easy dessert to give a well set mousse. Instead of using fresh fruit, you could use frozen berries – keep a packet in the freezer.

1 Blitz the strawberries in a blender and then add the tofu, a little at a time.

2 When it's really thick, add the maple syrup and blend until smooth.

3 Divide between 4 small bowls and chill in the fridge for 3–4 hours or overnight.

4 Before serving, sprinkle with the chocolate shavings and decorate with whole strawberries.

OR YOU CAN TRY THIS...
– Add a few drops of vanilla extract.
– If you prefer a tangy flavour, add 1–2 tablespoons lemon juice.
– Use agave syrup or clear honey to sweeten the mousse instead of maple syrup.

TOFU LEMON POTS

SERVES: 4 | **PREP:** 10 MINUTES | **CHILL:** 1 HOUR

350g/12oz silken tofu,
    drained
grated zest and juice of
    1 small lemon
a few drops of lemon extract
1 tbsp powdered coconut
    palm sugar
shredded or flaked coconut
    or lemon zest and finely
    chopped pistachios, to
    decorate

Silken tofu blends so well and makes a delicious, creamy and smooth high-protein dessert. Keep a packet in the cupboard for when you need to whip up a quick dessert. Once opened, it will stay fresh for up to five days in the fridge.

1 Put the tofu in a blender and blitz until creamy and smooth. Add the lemon zest and juice, lemon extract and coconut palm sugar and blitz briefly to combine.

2 Spoon the mixture into 4 small pots or ramekins and chill in the fridge for at least 1 hour.

3 To serve, decorate with grated coconut or lemon zest and chopped pistachios.

OR YOU CAN TRY THIS...
– Use agave syrup instead of coconut palm sugar.
– Instead of lemon, use the grated zest and juice of ½ orange and some orange extract.

CHOCOLATE, CHILLI & ORANGE POTS

SERVES: 4 | **PREP:** 15 MINUTES | **COOK:** 5 MINUTES | **CHILL:** 30 MINUTES

150g/5oz dark (bittersweet) chocolate, minimum 70% cocoa solids
450g/1lb silken tofu, drained
100ml/3½fl oz (⅓ cup) maple syrup
grated zest of 1 orange
2 tbsp orange juice
1 tsp ground cinnamon
a pinch of dried chilli flakes, crushed
a pinch of coarse sea salt
slivers of orange zest or chocolate shavings, to decorate

Chocolate and chilli are a surprisingly good combination, and cinnamon adds a warm spicy flavour to these little pots. Make sure you drain the tofu well, squeezing out as much liquid as possible.

1 Break the chocolate into pieces and place in a heatproof bowl suspended over a pan of simmering water. Leave until the chocolate melts, stirring occasionally, and remove from the heat.

2 Blitz the tofu, maple syrup, orange zest and juice, cinnamon, chilli flakes and salt in a blender or food processor until smooth and creamy. Add the melted chocolate and blitz briefly until well mixed and smooth.

3 Spoon the mixture into 4 small pots, ramekins or glass bowls. Chill in the fridge for at least 30 minutes until set.

4 Serve the pots, sprinkled with orange zest or grated chocolate.

OR YOU CAN TRY THIS...
– Use chilli powder instead of flakes.
– Substitute agave syrup for the maple syrup.
– Add a few drops of vanilla extract.

STICKY VEGAN TOFU BROWNIES

MAKES: 16 BROWNIES | **PREP:** 15 MINUTES | **COOK:** 35 MINUTES

300g/10oz silken tofu,
   drained
225g/8oz (1 cup)
   demerara sugar
120ml/4fl oz (½ cup)
   vegetable oil, e.g.
   sunflower, plus extra
   for brushing
4 tbsp cocoa powder
200g/7oz dark (bittersweet)
   chocolate, minimum
   70% cocoa solids
85g/3oz (¾ cup)
   self-raising
   (self-rising) flour
½ tsp baking powder
a pinch of coarse sea salt
1 tsp ground cinnamon
a few drops of vanilla
   extract
60g/2oz (½ cup)
   chopped walnuts
icing (confectioner's)
   sugar, for dusting

These delicious brownies are crisp on the outside and squidgy on the inside – nobody would ever guess that they are made with tofu! Enjoy them as a snack or serve for dessert with fresh fruit and dairy-free yoghurt alternative or cashew cream.

1 Preheat the oven to 180°C, 350°F, gas mark 4. Lightly brush a 20cm/8in square baking tin (pan) with oil and line with baking parchment.

2 Beat the tofu for 2–3 minutes in a food mixer or processor. Alternatively, use a hand-held electric whisk. Stir in the sugar, oil and cocoa powder, mixing well.

3 Break the chocolate into pieces and place in a heatproof bowl suspended over a pan of simmering water. Leave until the chocolate melts, stirring occasionally, and remove from the heat.

4 Gently stir the melted chocolate into the tofu mixture, and then fold in the flour, baking powder, salt, cinnamon and vanilla until everything is well combined. Stir in the walnuts, distributing them evenly throughout the mixture.

5 Spoon the mixture into the prepared baking tin, pushing it into the corners, and level the top with the back of a spoon. Bake for 35 minutes until risen and crusty on top and round the edges. Insert a metal skewer into the centre – if it comes out clean, the brownies are cooked.

6 Leave to cool in the tin for at least 1 hour, before dusting the top with icing sugar. Cut into 16 squares and remove from the tin. The brownies will keep well for up to 5 days, stored in an airtight container.

OR YOU CAN TRY THIS...
– Use chopped hazelnuts or pecans instead of walnuts.
– Add some almond extract, grated orange zest or crushed dried chilli flakes.

VEGAN TOFU CARROT CAKE

MAKES: 16 SQUARES | **PREP:** 15 MINUTES | **COOK:** 40-45 MINUTES

300g/10oz silken tofu
175g/6oz (¾ cup) demerara
    or granulated sugar
180ml/6fl oz (¾ cup)
    sunflower oil, plus
    extra for brushing
225g/8oz (4 cups) grated
    carrot
grated zest of 1 orange
175g/6oz (1¾ cups)
    self-raising (self-rising)
    flour, sifted
1 tsp baking powder
1 tsp ground cinnamon
½ tsp freshly grated nutmeg

For the frosting:
175g/6oz (1½ cups) icing
    (confectioner's) sugar
2-3 tbsp fresh orange juice

This vegan carrot cake is wonderfully moist and so quick and easy to make. If you don't want to make the frosting, it tastes good without it – just sprinkle a little sugar over the top.

1 Preheat the oven to 180°C, 350°F, gas mark 4. Lightly brush a 20cm/8in square baking tin (pan) with oil and line with baking parchment.

2 Beat the tofu for 2–3 minutes in a food mixer or processor. Alternatively, use a hand-held electric whisk. Beat in the sugar, oil, grated carrot and orange zest.

3 Gently fold in the flour, baking powder and spices until everything is well combined.

4 Spoon the mixture into the prepared baking tin, pushing it into the corners, and level the top with the back of a spoon. Bake for 40–45 minutes until risen and firm. Insert a metal skewer into the centre – if it comes out clean, the cake is cooked. Leave in the tin to cool.

5 For the frosting, sift the icing sugar into a bowl and stir in enough orange juice to make an icing that will coat the back of a spoon.

6 Pour the frosting over the cold cake and when it's set, cut into 16 squares. The cake will keep well for up to 5 days, stored in an airtight container in the fridge.

OR YOU CAN TRY THIS...
– Flavour the cake with vanilla extract and ground cloves.
– Add some raisins or chopped macadamia nuts.
– Sprinkle the cake with slivers of orange zest.

10 9 8 7 6 5 4 3 2 1

Published in 2019 by Ebury Press an imprint of Ebury Publishing,
20 Vauxhall Bridge Road,
London SW1V 2SA

Ebury Press is part of the Penguin Random House group of companies
whose addresses can be found at global.penguinrandomhouse.com

Penguin
Random House
UK

Design: Louise Evans
Photography: Joff Lee
Food stylist: Mari Williams
Editor: Sam Crisp

First published by Ebury Press in 2019

www.penguin.co.uk

A CIP catalogue record for this book is available from the British Library

ISBN 9781529104394

Printed and bound in China by C&C Offset Printing Co., Ltd